Revitalizing Catholicism in America

Revitalizing Catholicism in America

Nine Tasks for Every Catholic

Russell Shaw
David Byers

Our Sunday Visitor
Huntington, Indiana

Nihil Obstat
Msgr. Michael Heintz, Ph.D.
Censor Librorum

Imprimatur
✠ Kevin C. Rhoades
Bishop of Fort Wayne-South Bend
January 16, 2023

The *Nihil Obstat* and *Imprimatur* are official declarations that a book is free from doctrinal or moral error. It is not implied that those who have granted the *Nihil Obstat* and *Imprimatur* agree with the contents, opinions, or statements expressed.

Except where noted, the Scripture citations used in this work are taken from the *Revised Standard Version of the Bible — Second Catholic Edition*, copyright © 1965, 1966, 2006 National Council of the Churches of Christ in the United States of America. Used by permission. All rights reserved.

Every reasonable effort has been made to determine copyright holders of excerpted materials and to secure permissions as needed. If any copyrighted materials have been inadvertently used in this work without proper credit being given in one form or another, please notify Our Sunday Visitor in writing so that future printings of this work may be corrected accordingly.

Our Sunday Visitor Publishing Division
Our Sunday Visitor, Inc.
200 Noll Plaza
Huntington, IN 46750
www.osv.com
1-800-348-2440

ISBN: 978-1-63966-006-3 (Inventory No. T2747)
1. RELIGION—Christianity—Catholic.
2. RELIGION—Christian Living—Social Issues.
3. RELIGION—Christian Living—General.

eISBN: 978-1-63966-007-0
LCCN: 2023933568

Cover design and Interior design: Amanda Falk
Cover art: AdobeStock

Printed in the United States of America

Contents

— 1 —

Why the Laity Must Save the Church

*The Church would look
foolish without them.*

— St. John Henry Newman

Here are two simple statements, one indisputable and the other ... well, let's see.

First, the Catholic Church in the United States is in a very serious crisis. The crisis is painfully visible in the sharp declines that have already taken place in many essential areas of Church life, from Catholic marriages to infant baptisms, from the rate of Sunday Mass attendance to the number of priests, and much, very much, besides.

While you're absorbing that, here is the second statement: The Catholic laity need to step up and save the Church.

"Hold on," a not-too-friendly critic might break in here. "I can't swallow that. I admit the truth of what you say about a crisis, and I could even add a few examples that you didn't mention. So the signs of decline in the Church since the 1960s are admittedly disturbing. But I don't see how you can expect the laity to save the Church. Maybe we can help here and there, but the pope and the bishops and the priests make all the important decisions. We lay people just have to stand by and watch — and hope for the best."

The objection itself unconsciously illustrates one serious obstacle — the clericalism that affects so many Catholics. And not just the clergy either, but especially the laity, who use their seemingly subordinate position in the Church as an excuse for remaining passive in the face of the present crisis. We shall have much more to say about clericalism, especially its lay variety, later in this book. But first let's lay to rest the notion that lay people can only stand on the sidelines and watch the crisis unfold.

For one thing, the Catholic laity collectively make many important decisions that shape the Church for better or worse already. For instance: lay people decide to contribute or not contribute money and time to the Church, to attend or not attend Mass regularly, to participate or not participate in parish and diocesan activities, to send or not send their children to Catholic schools. And so on. Examples could be multiplied, but the point should be clear: The laity can't plead helplessness. They have great latent power if they choose to use it, and they can't let themselves off the hook by claiming that they never decide anything important for the Church. By what they choose to do

— or not do, for that matter —, the laity already are shaping the Church in many important ways.

Historically, moreover, the laity made a major contribution to saving the Church in the face of at least one huge crisis in the past. So, leaving aside our timidity and our laziness, what is to say that what happened before couldn't happen again?

"'Happened before?' I repeat — you can't be serious."

Quite serious. Just as serious as St. John Henry Newman was in describing the Church's response to the Arian heresy in the fourth century. Arianism was a Christian heresy which asserted that Christ did not have a divine nature but was only a very remarkable human being and nothing more. Here was a heresy that denied one of the fundamentals of our faith, the Incarnation — the doctrine that for the sake of our redemption the Second Person of the Holy Trinity took on human nature while retaining his Divine Nature. And yet by the fourth century, Arianism, a heresy contrary to that dogma, was widely accepted by bishops and priests and seemed on its way to becoming the established, official version of Christianity.

This was the context in AD 325 in which the Council of Nicaea, the first ecumenical council of the Church, taught clearly and firmly that Christ was of one divine substance with the Father. As a practical matter, however, even that didn't settle things. Arianism persisted and, if anything, grew even stronger in the years after Nicaea, while some bishops and clergy waffled — or worse. Here is Newman's account:

> I mean … that in that time of immense confusion the divine dogma of our Lord's divinity was proclaimed, enforced, maintained, and (humanly speaking), preserved, far more by the *Ecclesia docta* [the portion of the Church that is taught — that is, the laity] than by the *Ecclesia docens* [the portion of the Church responsible for

teaching — the bishops and clergy]; that the body of the episcopate was unfaithful to its commission, while the body of the laity was faithful to its baptism; that at one time the Pope, at other times the patriarchal, metropolitan, and other great sees, at other times general councils, said what they should not have said, or did what obscured and compromised revealed truth; while, on the other hand, it was the Christian people who, under Providence, were the ecclesiastical strength of Athanasius, Hilary, Eusebius of Verecellae, and other great solitary confessors, who would have failed without them.[1]

To be sure, as Newman notes, the faithful laity were taught and led by faithful bishops and teachers during the six decades of "controversy and disorder" that followed the Council of Nicaea. But in the end, he maintains, it was "the faithful whose loyal perseverance decided it."[2] Although Arianism lingered for the next several centuries, the fundamental doctrine of the Incarnation had been vindicated, proclaimed, and upheld as the authentic faith of the Church, thanks in no small part to the laity's persistence in standing by that faith.

Newman's commentary, published originally in July 1859 in a journal called *The Rambler* (it was republished twelve years later as an appendix to his historical study of Arianism), earned him no friends in British Catholic clerical circles, and also raised hackles in Rome. Today, though, his words stand as a bold and enlightened analysis of a phenomenon relevant to our own troubled times: In the face of the huge crisis occasioned by the spread of Arianism, the Catholic laity saved the Church.

"But in the end," our skeptic might say, "it was the doing of the Holy Spirit, wasn't it?"

Certainly it was. The Spirit's action was indispensable then just as it is now. But, as is usually the case, the Spirit acted in and by means of the cooperation of human beings — in this instance, the Catholic laity and the faithful bishops and theologians whom they supported.

What lay people did then, lay people can do now — although the challenge today is clearly very different from, and in some ways more threatening than, a single great heresy like Arianism. For today Christianity is not challenged by a single heresy but by a devil's stew of hostile mindsets and aberrant behaviors, all coming together under an umbrella called *secularization* and producing deeply disturbing results.

Consider the numbers. Just 5% of Americans were religiously unaffiliated in the early 1970s, but by 2022 the unaffiliated had soared to 30% of the population. "In a field where shifts typically move at a glacial pace," says a Baptist pastor, "that demographic factoid may represent the most abrupt and most consequential shift in American society in the postwar period."[3] Along with other religious bodies, the Catholic Church has been part of this process of contraction and decline, as we shall show in detail later. And it is from this process that lay people now are called to save the Church — the Christian Church in general and, for the purposes of this book, the Catholic Church in particular.

In revitalizing the Church, moreover, we need to find our own way, not rely on a model from the fourth century or any era before this one. To be passive is to surrender. Indifference and waiting for instructions from on high could be fatal. Today's Catholic lay people need to recognize the Church in her historical reality, evaluate her in light of traditional Christian standards, and help carry her forward toward survival and renewal under the guidance of the Holy Spirit.

A detailed study of recent giving in a number of religious denominations in the United States draws the obvious conclusion: "The religious impulse is weakening in both church giving and membership. ... Those who love the church and its calling are faced with the task of figuring out what to do. ... To choose not to do anything is still to choose."[4] That conviction informs the diagnosis and prescription of this book.

• • •

At the outset, we need to set the scene with a quick scan of history. If it does nothing else, the overview that follows should make it clear that the present crisis (which, we repeat, is a crisis not only of Catholicism but of organized religion in general throughout much of the West) has deep historical roots. To think otherwise — to suppose that the causes of the crisis, like the crisis itself, are of recent vintage — not only would impoverish our grasp of the situation we face but also could encourage the delusion that this is just a momentary glitch that will fade quickly without requiring any special effort on our part.

It is entirely possible that the present crisis is the most serious the Catholic Church has faced since the Reformation in the sixteenth century. In fact, it is not impossible that it will prove to be even more serious than the Reformation. For although the religious clashes of those days shattered the unity of Christendom, in doing so they also created what historian Brad S. Gregory calls "a firm launching pad for ideological and institutional secularization" such as we are now experiencing.[5] And secularization, philosopher Charles Taylor remarks, is a fundamental transformation in the way people understand the world and their place in it — a shift "from a condition in which belief was the default option...to a condition in which for more and more people unbelieving construals [Taylor's word for interpretations] seem at first blush the only plausible ones."[6]

Not surprisingly, however, what happened took place in stages extending over several centuries. Hard on the heels of the Reformation and the wars of religion came the seventeenth and eighteenth centuries' Age of Enlightenment. Celebrated in secularist circles today as a historic breakthrough, the era of Voltaire and the *philosophes* was viewed with realistic reservations by religious believers close to the event. Writing in 1836, for example, Orestes Brownson, a convert to Catholicism who was the leading American Catholic public intellectual of his day, remarked that what had passed during the previous hundred years for "the intelligence of the world" had by his day become "divorced from orthodoxy."

> During this period the most successful cultivators of science, of history, literature, and art, have not been Catholics, or, if nominally Catholics, with little understanding of the teaching, or devotion to the practice, of the church. The natural sciences, zoology, geology, chemistry, natural history, ethnography, metaphysics, and to some extent history itself, have been anti-Catholic, while the popular literature, that which takes hold of the heart and forms the taste, the mind, and the morals of a nation, has been decidedly hostile to the church.[7]

Since then, of course, Catholic participation in many, though not all, of the fields Brownson mentions has experienced a gratifying rebirth. Yet orthodox Catholics still not infrequently find themselves to be targets of hostile discrimination. And not only Catholics. Evangelical scholar Carl R. Trueman writes that "the Enlightenment did not simply rebel against old ways of thinking about knowledge; it rebelled also against the moral teachings of Christianity." And the Enlightenment rebelled with results both visible and unpleasant: "Today's cultural despisers of Christianity do not find its teachings to be intellectually implausible; they regard them as morally reprehensible. … Failure to conform to new orthodoxies on race, morality, sexual orientation, and gender identity is the main reason orthodox Christianity is despised today."[8]

For people of faith, the demystification that Charles Taylor describes as intrinsic to the secularization process of the past half millennium is welcome insofar as it replaced conjecture and magical thinking with a growing objective understanding of nature and humanity. At the same time, however, this new view of reality came with its own ideological baggage, including *a priori* assumptions and attitudes antagonistic to ways of thinking and acting shaped by religious faith.

Prominent among these new mindsets is exaggerated individualism. And here two figures in particular stand out: Martin Luther (1483–1546) and Jean-Jacques Rousseau (1712–78).

Early on, Luther's overwrought emphasis concentrated on the isolated, guilt-ridden self, standing alone under the relentless gaze of an all-seeing, ever-judging God; but the Luther of later years basked in a self-centered version of faith that situated Martin, in his self-regarding singularity, within the scope of redeeming grace. In both phases taken together, Luther is, in Jacques Maritain's words, "the very type of modern individualism."[9] For Luther, writes Alasdair MacIntyre, "the true transformation of the individual is entirely internal; to be before God in fear and trembling as a justified sinner is what matters."[10] And still more, argues German theologian Paul Hacker, the crucial heart of justification according to Luther is "not simply faith in God or Christ [but] the reflection, qualified by certitude, that God's salvific deed is meant '*for me*'."[11] Here, says Hacker, is "the seed of anthropocentrism in religion" — the human self replacing God at center stage in the great drama of religious faith, acted out, for instance, in religious services in which the focus is on the presider and the congregation rather than the One to whom the act of worship is presumably directed.[12]

Jean-Jacques Rousseau is certainly very different from Mar-

tin Luther, but he is hardly less centered on the self. In the person
of Rousseau, the Enlightenment, with its vaunted emphasis on
rationality, reaches its ironic culmination in the all-important
individual who is the very personification of subjectivism and
feeling. Says Maritain: "'You must be yourself'; in the last years
of his life Jean-Jacques liked to repeat this formula. On his lips it
meant: you must *be* your feeling. ... You must regard as sin every
attempt to form yourself, or allow yourself to be formed, to right
yourself, to bring your discords to unity again."[13] Here is the pro-
totype and model of 1960s- and 1970s-style individualism and
its gospel of 'let it all hang out' in unconstrained gratification of
the all-important self.

We find another aspect of the mindset of secularism at work
in Luther's and Rousseau's views on political life and governance.
Luther boasted of upholding the absolute rights of secular authority, a stance that amounted, MacIntyre says, to "handing
over the secular world to its own devices."[14] The results for political morality have been predictably disastrous. A different dynamic, but with consequences no less troubling, can be seen in
Rousseau's strong concern for the right ordering of political life.
While identifying the "common will" as the appropriate norm for
shaping and maintaining a just, virtuous society, Rousseau held
that most members of the more or less corrupt society of his day
(or any day, for that matter) could not be trusted to recognize
and carry out the common will. Therefore, this so-important
task was to be entrusted to "the minority of the virtuous," who,
acting in their self-anointed capacity as "vehicles of the genuine
common will," would organize society according to their lights.[15]

Does that sound familiar? It should. It is the formula of *virtuous tyranny* — an ideal whose fruits, Charles Taylor observes,
could soon be seen on display in the blood-drenched killing
spree that marked the Jacobin phase of the French Revolution
and were later "continued ... in Leninist Communism."[16] Today

the same mindset of virtuous tyranny is at work — in aspiration if not yet in fully realized fact — in the cancel culture of Western cultural elites busying themselves on behalf of transgenderism and critical race theory, along with earlier favorites like legalized abortion and same-sex marriage, as components of their project for shaping a social order to their liking.[17]

In the nineteenth century, the phenomenon of *disenchantment* — Taylor's word for the abandonment of a world view undergirded by religion (and also, it must be admitted, by a residue of magical thinking) moved ahead hand in hand with secularization, drawing more and more people away from traditional beliefs. Darwinism and evolution did not create this dynamic, but they unquestionably gave "an important push towards a materialist, reductive view of the cosmos" from which any sense of divine agency had been purged.[18] The result found notable literary expression in Matthew Arnold's poem "Dover Beach" with its elegiac picture of a world from which the "Sea of Faith" had withdrawn, leaving behind "neither joy, nor love, nor light / Nor certitude, nor peace, nor help for pain."[19]

There is a touching cameo account of this process at work within one family in Edmund Gosse's minor classic *Father and Son*. Gosse, now largely forgotten but a prominent British literary figure of the Edwardian era, was the only child of parents who were devout members of the Plymouth Brethren, a fundamentalist Protestant sect that identified orthodoxy with an ultra-literal reading of the Bible, including the story of creation as found in the book of Genesis.

For biblical fundamentalists like the elder Gosses, the theory of evolution posed a deadly threat. Responding to that challenge, Edmund's father Philip Gosse, a successful writer of works of popular naturalism, stood by his religious convictions and even published a book called *Omphalos* — Greek mythology's name for the supposed center and point of origin of the earth — in which he argued against the fossil evidence of evolution and maintained that God had created living creatures, including human beings, in their mature, fully developed form. Predictably, young Edmund soon abandoned his parents' faith, thereby moving father to write son a heartfelt letter deploring this "horrid, insidious infidelity ... sapping the very foundations of faith, on which all true godliness, all real religion, must rest." But the son was not persuaded, "and thus desperately challenged ... threw off once for all the yoke of his 'dedication', and, as respectfully as he could, without parade or remonstrance, he took a human being's privilege to fashion his inner life for himself."[20]

The rise of liberal Protestantism reflected a reaction to scientific naturalism profoundly different from Philip Gosse's fundamentalism. Drawing on nineteenth century German biblical scholarship that seemed to undermine the historicity of Scripture, liberal Protestants sought a *modus vivendi* with the spirit of the age in a watered-down Christianity that asked little of adherents in the way of belief. A few decades later something similar emerged in Catholicism in the form of the "Modernism" that Pope St. Pius X condemned in his 1907 encyclical *Pascendi Dominici Gregis* (Feeding the Lord's Flock).[21]

Literary gentlemen like Matthew Arnold and Edmund Gosse wrote of the loss of faith in genteel, wistful terms. But in Germany, Friedrich Nietzsche went far beyond the boundaries of conventional secularism and delivered his half-mad rant against Christianity with something approaching demonic vehemence, as in this passage from *Ecce Homo*, a volume that Nietzsche's family withheld from print until after his death in 1900:

The concept of "God" invented as a counterconcept of life — everything harmful, poisonous, slanderous, the whole hostility unto death against life synthesized in this concept in a gruesome unity! The concept of the

"beyond," the "true world" invented in order to devalu-
ate the only world there is — in order to retain no goal,
no reason, no task for our earthly reality! The concept
of the "soul," the "spirit," finally even "*immortal* soul,"
invented in order to despise the body, to make it sick,
"holy"; to oppose with a ghastly levity everything that
deserves to be taken seriously in life.[22]

Scholars disagree on how much influence Nietzsche had on
Adolf Hitler, but however great or little it may have been, the
Führer certainly professed admiration for Nietzsche, borrowed
ideas and turns of speech from his writings, had himself photo-
graphed next to a bust of Nietzsche while visiting the Nietzsche
archive in Weimar,[23] and gave a set of Nietzsche's works to Italian
dictator Benito Mussolini for his birthday.[24] Pope St. John Paul
II may have had Nietzsche in mind in 1986 when, speaking of
modern atheism in his encyclical on the Holy Spirit, he wrote: "It
follows, according to this interpretation, that religion can only be
understood as a kind of 'idealistic illusion,' to be fought with the
most suitable means and methods according to circumstances
of time and place, in order to eliminate it from society and from
man's very heart."[25] An apt description not only of Nietzsche but
of the goals and methods of today's not-so-new "New Atheists"
as well.

As the Sea of Faith receded in Europe, it also declined among
elites in America. Henry Adams, great-grandson of one president and grandson of another, recorded the process as he experienced it while growing up in the middle years of the nineteenth
century. The Unitarian clergymen of Boston were admirable
gentlemen, he wrote in his autobiographical work *The Education
of Henry Adams*, but nothing in their preaching expressed or in-
stilled living faith, so that by an early age "the religious instinct
had vanished and could not be revived."

The boy went to church twice every Sunday; he was taught to read his Bible, and he learned religious poetry by heart; he believed in a mild deism; he prayed; he went through all the forms; but neither to him nor to his brothers or sisters was religion real. Even the mild discipline of the Unitarian Church was so irksome that they all threw it off at the first possible moment, and never afterwards entered a church.[26]

As a matter of fact, in the sad later years following his wife's suicide during one of her episodes of depression, Henry Adams did enter churches, indeed quite a few of them, perhaps half-seeking the faith he'd never possessed yet somehow felt he had lost. Meanwhile the infection of disbelief that had begun with elitists like Adams filtered downward into other, less rarefied strata of American society.

Over the years, that disbelief has taken different forms, including variations on the theme of radical, subjective individualism sounded by the 1950s beatniks, the 1960s hippies, and eventually by no less than three members of the United States Supreme Court. In 1992, Associate Justices Anthony Kennedy, Sandra Day O'Connor, and David Souter made radical individualism the centerpiece of their argument in a key case affirming the right to abortion. Citing the "private realm of family life" and "the most intimate and personal choices a person may make," the three proclaimed this individualist dogma: "At the heart of liberty is the right to define one's own concept of existence, of meaning, of the universe, and of the mystery of human life."[27] And, we must add, a right not just to "define" life's meaning, but to destroy nascent human life for the sake of pursuing "one's own concept of existence" at the expense of the existence of someone not allowed to have a say in the matter.

Of course the justices did not think of it this way; undoubtedly they saw themselves as being tolerant and inclusive and commendably right-thinking. Time and again, such bland blindness to reality has borne out Alasdair MacIntyre's observation that "modern society is ... nothing but a collection of strangers, each pursuing his or her own interests under minimal constraints" as well as his mordant conclusion: "Modern politics is civil war carried on by other means."[28]

And in this confused, ever so civilized, shockingly brutal setting — American secularist culture in the twenty-first century — the Catholic laity must set to work revitalizing and thereby saving their Church.

In what follows we shall explain how lay people need to approach that task, which necessarily will involve holding and offering to others a view of the world, of human life, and of our relationship to the Creator profoundly different from the philosobabble of three Supreme Court justices. First, though, realizing that, as we've already seen, skepticism is likely to greet the claim that the laity must save the Church, we recall something else John Henry Newman said.

Newman came under fire for his views on consulting the laity, which he had illustrated by the example of the lay response to the Arian heresy in the fourth century. One result of the controversy that followed publication of his article was a polite, slightly strained conversation with his bishop, the sympathetic but not always comprehending W.B. Ullathorne. At one point, Ullathorne posed a rhetorical question: "Who are the laity?" To which, Newman later recalled, he responded in some such words as these: "The Church would look foolish without them."[29]

We recall this celebrated incident in order to make a simple, self-evident point — one that, nevertheless, is still sometimes overlooked by Catholics: The laity are far, far and away the largest part of the Catholic Church. That has consequences that can perhaps best be stated negatively: If Catholic laywomen and men do not rise to the challenge of being actively, intimately involved in bringing American Catholicism safe and whole through this present crisis, the Church will be at risk of being overwhelmed by hostile cultural forces that threaten her very survival.

This book is a modest attempt to explain what "actively, intimately involved" can and must mean today.

— 2 —

The American Church
Growth and Decline

She blossoms like the rose.
— Cardinal James Gibbons

It was March 25, 1887. Observing a custom dating back to the days when cardinals were the pastors of Rome's principal churches, Cardinal James Gibbons of Baltimore, newly installed in the College of Cardinals, was taking formal possession of his "titular" Roman church, the venerable Santa Maria in Trastevere, located a short distance from the Vatican. He used the occasion to deliver a homily that contemporaries, aware of Vatican sensitivities, regarded as a bold statement for so habitually cautious a man as Gibbons.

The potential red flag in the new cardinal's remarks had complex origins. In part it reflected the Holy See's strained relations with the anticlerical governments then in power in Italy, Germany, and France — a state of affairs that fed Rome's already skeptical view of Catholic prospects in the United States. For here, an ocean away, was a young country not only democratic in government and religiously pluralistic in population but also culturally Protestant in fact. The Constitution decreed church and state separate — a doctrine in conflict with the view long favored by Catholic theorists and papal pronouncements, that formal recognition of Catholicism as a country's official, established religion was desirable and, where possible, natural.

Considering all this, there really was something provocative about the new cardinal's words that day:

> Our Holy Father, Leo XIII, in his luminous encyclical on the constitution of Christian States [*Immortale Dei*, November 1, 1885], declares that the Church is not committed to any particular form of civil government. … She has lived under absolute empires; she thrives under constitutional monarchies; she grows and expands under the free republic. She has often, indeed, been hampered in her divine mission and has had to struggle for a footing wherever despotism has cast its dark shadow like the plant excluded from the sunlight, but in the genial air of liberty she blossoms like the rose!

Lest anyone miss his meaning, Gibbons went on to express "pride and gratitude" at living in a nation "where the civil government holds over us the aegis of its protection without interfering in the legitimate exercise of our sublime mission as ministers of the

Gospel of Jesus Christ."[1]

Together with other fervent Americanizers in the American hierarchy such as Archbishop John Ireland of St. Paul and Bishop John Keane of Richmond, first rector of The Catholic University of America, Gibbons championed the cultural assimilation of Catholics, many of them immigrants or the children of immigrants, into the nation's mainstream. The Americanizers' cause suffered a momentary setback in 1899 when Leo XIII in his letter *Testem Benevolentiae* unequivocally condemned a heresy he called Americanism,[2] but, despite that, the assimilation project itself went on undeterred in the years that followed.

Even so, due largely to the lay trustee controversy in which recalcitrant American laymen challenged episcopal authority (more on that later), the enthusiasm of men like Gibbons and Ireland for American-style democracy ended at the church door. The actual situation of the Catholic laity at this time is suggested by the fact that when prominent laymen, including one of Orestes Brownson's sons, sought the bishops' approval in 1889 for a national lay congress, permission was forthcoming only on the condition that papers intended for delivery there be submitted first to a committee of bishops for approval.[3]

The Americanizers' enthusiasm for their country's religious arrangement also existed in unavoidable tension with the historic reality of American anti-Catholicism. As had been the case for many years, the Catholic Church in nineteenth-century America was widely disliked and viewed with suspicion. Lurid anti-Catholic propaganda circulated freely. Earlier in the century, Protestant ministers had written *The Awful Disclosures of Maria Monk*, published in 1835 and purporting to be the work of an ex-nun. Reaction against Catholic immigration from Ireland and Germany spurred the formation of the Native American Party — better known as the "Know-Nothings" — in 1844. Anti-Catholic riots and church burnings took place in several places, notably Philadelphia in May and July of 1844. Picking up where the Know-Nothings left off, the specifically anti-Catholic and secretive American Protective Association flourished briefly, especially in the Midwest, during the century's latter years.

• • •

Considered against this background, the pros and cons of Catholic assimilation require some important distinctions. For one thing, while agreeing that assimilation was desirable, different nationality groups held different views on its ideal pace, with the Irish favoring speed and the Germans favoring a go-slow approach. It is likewise important to realize that, in the face of virulent anti-Catholicism, assimilation for American Catholics did not mean passive absorption into the surrounding culture but a process whose underlying attitude might be summed up as, "Assimilation, yes, but on our own terms." Although deeply appreciative of their nation's many values and virtues, Catholics were determined to retain their cherished religious identity — a commitment that expressed itself in weekly Sunday Mass attendance, eating fish on Fridays, a focus on parish life, and attendance at Catholic elementary and secondary schools.

As we turn now to the twentieth century, these schools deserve particular attention.

Parochial schools had been strongly endorsed by the American bishops at three Plenary Councils of Baltimore in 1852, 1866, and 1884. The third council, with Cardinal Gibbons presiding, declared in Title VI of its decrees that pastors should establish parish schools, that Catholic parents should send their children to them unless the local bishop agreed that there was sufficient reason for sending them elsewhere, and that the schools should, if possible, be free. By 1900, Catholic elementary and secondary schools in the United States numbered over 3,800 and enrolled more than 850,000 children and young people.[4] In 1965, these numbers reached a highwater mark of 13,300 schools and 5.6 million students.[5]

The creation of the Catholic school system was an extraordinary achievement, and teaching sisters were at the heart of it. Many of today's older Catholics recall with a mixture of affection and awe the sisters who taught them and, later, their children. Let Sr. Agnes Gertrude, a Sister of Charity assigned in the 1950s to Corpus Christi School in Hasbrouck Heights, New Jersey, stand for this body of remarkable women.

Sr. Agnes Gertrude taught sixty first-graders in one room, a heroic feat even in those days of automatic respect for sisters and priests. She was short and plump, floated among her young charges like a blessing, maintained order effortlessly, and never lost her temper — not even when a boy ate half a dark blue crayon and then, realizing what he'd done, wailed in terror. She was marvelous, and all that a sister should be. She died one night in her sleep, not yet thirty years of age. Corpus Christi School grieved intensely, unwilling to let her go, and nursed its pain for the rest of the school year.

If assimilation was of central importance to the rise of American Catholicism, so also was the special quality of Catholic identity as it was lived in places like Corpus Christi School by people like Sr. Agnes Gertrude. By the early years of the twentieth century, this identity extended throughout a thriving Catholic subculture organized around a network of specifically Catholic institutions and groups — schools from the elementary level through the university, hospitals, social service agencies, publishing houses producing and distributing periodicals and books of all sorts, organizations for particular groups from children and young people to physicians and philosophers.

Situated at the heart of the Catholic subculture was the ever-growing number of parishes, many established to serve the needs of particular nationalities — Germans, Italians, Poles, Slovaks — and each with its own cluster of organizations for particular groups: pious women (Sodality of Our Lady, Altar and Rosary Society), adult men (Holy Name Society, Knights of Columbus), and pre-teens and adolescents interested in sports and/or socials (Catholic Youth Organization).

At its apex in the 1940s and 1950s, recalls historian Charles R. Morris, the American Catholic subculture was "a virtual state-within-a-state [within which] Catholics could live almost their entire lives." Yet this state-within-a-state, besides providing powerful support to Catholic identity, also helped foster the rise of Catholics in American life — so much so that, as Morris points out, "by the mid-twentieth century, the Church had managed to become a dominant cultural force."[6]

At this time, too, America was assuming a new role as the world's sole superpower. As possessor of the atomic bomb — the only nation with that awesome weapon — and a powerful economy, the United States emerged from World War II with a sense of itself as the providentially chosen champion of democracy. Soon, this national self-image was reinforced by the onset of the Cold War, Soviet domination of Eastern Europe behind the shield of an Iron Curtain, and the Korean conflict. In this all-fronts global confrontation, America was the leader of the free world with a God-given mission to battle an atheistic opponent on behalf of democracy and religion.

Not surprisingly, then, these were boom times for American religion. World War II had fostered the homogenization of religious sensibilities as people of diverse faiths made common cause fighting and defeating the nation's enemies, and now the postwar struggle with "godless communism" further enhanced this sense of common purpose within the religious community. There was wide and happy recognition that the spiritual core of what many had previously considered an essentially Protestant nation could now be summed up accurately as "Protestant, Catholic, Jew." Figures like Archbishop Fulton Sheen and Rabbi Abraham Joshua Heschel joined Protestants like Norman Vincent Peale and Billy Graham as universally respected religious leaders commanding a national audience.

Catholics felt intellectually and emotionally at home in this setting, and Hollywood accommodated them with friendly, thoroughly Catholic films: the Bing Crosby-Barry Fitzgerald hit *Going My Way*, with Crosby as a crooning curate and Fitzgerald as a crusty but warm-hearted Irish pastor; *The Song of Bernadette*, an entirely respectful dramatic depiction of the apparitions of the Blessed Virgin at Lourdes; and *On the Waterfront*, with Karl Malden as a gutsy priest defending workers' rights. Best-selling books of the day included Thomas Merton's *The Seven Storey Mountain* — the autobiography of an intellectual and poet who became a Trappist monk — and Henry Morton Robinson's novel *The Cardinal*, a thinly veiled, highly romanticized fictionalization of the career of Cardinal Francis Spellman of New York. And of course — hard to imagine three-quarters of a century later — Bishop Sheen's *Life Is Worth Living,* a surprise hit of network television's early days, was widely viewed by Catholics and non-Catholics alike.

In this congenial environment, what the Catholic subculture mainly provided Catholics was a gratifying sense of their place, both in the divine scheme of things and in a well-defined human community. These two comforting certainties in turn mediated a third: the perception of Catholics' appropriate relationship to the world. The sense of security and contentment to which this certainty gave rise is suggested by the recollections of one of the present writers of how it felt to be an altar boy on Christmas Eve back then:

It's high drama when you're an altar boy at Midnight Mass and get to carry one of those little lighted lanterns on poles, and you and the guys on either side of you march in concert because the solemnity of the occasion rules out mistakes or misbehavior. The congregation — darkened shapes in the pews on either side of you as you move down the aisle in stately procession — stirs and shuffles its feet, coughs occasionally, and strains to get a look. With you at its head! Up in the loft, the choir has been singing Christmas hymns for a full fifteen minutes before the service, and now Miss Green launches into *O Holy Night*:

> The stars are brightly shining.
> It is the night of our dear Savior's birth.
> Till he appeared and the soul felt its worth.

At least one altar boy unquestionably is feeling his worth just then. And now the full choir joins in with a crash: "Fall on your knees!" The procession reaches the sanctuary, the church lights flash on, mimicking the hymn's celebration of "a new and glorious dawn." And surely, the boy supposes, this, like so much else in his experience of the faith, is just how the Church has always done it and always will keep on doing it for all time to come — *saecula saeculorum*!

Little did he and others like him suspect that in a few short years anonymous aliens called "liturgists," apparently unaware of and surely indifferent to the notably successful liturgical inculturation achieved by American Catholicism, would impose a very different style of worship (in English, with a celebrant facing the congregation, streamlined rubrics, and guitars strumming pseudo-folk songs) upon worshipers who hadn't asked for it and had felt at home with a dignified ritual celebrated in time-hallowed Latin.

But that was yet to come. For the present, nearly everything seemed to be coming up roses for the American Church. Possibly the only visible cloud on the horizon was the continued presence of pockets of anti-Catholicism. It had flared up, public and assertive, during Al Smith's 1928 presidential campaign and would soon reappear in John F. Kennedy's 1960 run for the White House. Between the Smith and Kennedy campaigns, anti-Catholicism received a veneer of intellectual respectability in *American Freedom and Catholic Power*, a 1949 volume by an associate editor of *The Nation* named Paul Blanshard.

Blanshard warned that the increasing social and political power of Catholics posed a threat to American democracy because of the essentially authoritarian nature of the Church as seen in countries where Catholics were in the ascendancy. The book sold well and caused a stir, but its chief significance may have been to highlight the growing influence of Catholics in American life. Catholics themselves angrily refuted Blanshard's thesis. Jesuit theologian John Courtney Murray argued eloquently that not only was the Church no threat to American values but the natural law/natural rights framework developed by Catholic thinkers was central to the American Founding itself. "The American political community was organized in an era when the tradition of natural law and natural rights was still vigorous," Murray wrote. "Claiming no sanction other than its appeal to free minds, it still commanded universal acceptance. And it furnished the basic materials for the American consensus."[7] Unfortunately, as he sadly acknowledged, by the time he wrote, the natural law tradition with its Catholic roots was already a dead letter in secular intellectual circles.[8]

• • •

And here perhaps may be a key to why the post-World War II religious boom eventually fizzled: Somehow or other, it appeared, America had already lost living contact with its founding roots, especially the religious ones. But if it had, that was not entirely new. As one recent commentator points out, the eighteenth century as a whole "saw declining religiosity in America, with the period of the American Revolution being a uniquely secular time."[9] Religious commitment in America had had its ups and downs ever since.

Granted the truth of that, it nevertheless is cold comfort now and surely no cause for complacency, as if the earlier renewals of fervor made religion's speedy recovery a certainty this time, too. For, as the same writer says of the present moment: "Obviously, something has changed since the 1960s. Religious affiliation is falling faster than ever before, to lower levels than have been seen at any point in American history."[10]

Moreover, the open hostility that now exists toward religion in general and Catholicism in particular is not confined to a relatively small number of elites and activists but reaches broadly into academia and media. This is without precedent in the American past and is a uniquely disturbing phenomenon of the present. In his widely discussed book *The Benedict Option*, conservative writer Rod Dreher holds that as matters now stand in the United States and other Western nations, people of faith "are living under barbarism. ... Our scientists, our judges, our princes, our scholars, and our scribes — they are at work demolishing the faith, the family, gender, even what it means to be human. Our barbarians have exchanged the animal pelts and spears of the past for designer suits and smartphones."[11] Both popular and elite culture have abandoned a relatively static God-centered worldview to embrace individualistic liberty and a general sloughing-off of old values and beliefs.

A literary precursor of this new mindset, J. D. Salinger's 1951 novel *The Catcher in the Rye*, preached an anti-authority message through the slangy monologue of an alienated teenager. Here was a prophetic holy book for the student revolt that erupted a decade later with devastating impact on college campuses. The revolt then spread rapidly amid mass orgies like Woodstock, accompanied by the wailing of folk singers and the smells of burning weed and tear gas; tragedies like Kent State; and the killings of John and Robert Kennedy and Dr. Martin Luther King. And all this against the background of a never-ending war in Vietnam.

Along with other institutions, America's churches were deeply affected by this moral bedlam. Clergy and laity, educated and ignorant, committed and lukewarm, all rushed to embrace full, unconditional assimilation, even as the faith identities of millions of American *Protestants and Catholics* wavered. Drawn by the gravitational pull of secular culture, they were transformed into weakly Protestant and Catholic *Americans*, adrift on seas of uncertainty and doubt.

Our particular concern here, however, is not the crisis of American religion in general but the crisis of Catholicism in particular. Although the Second Vatican Council (1962–65) and papal documents like Pope St. Paul VI's *Evangelii Nuntiandi* (1975) called on Catholics to evangelize the culture, very many Catholics were instead evangelized by a secular culture in the throes of cultural revolution. "The times they are a-changin,'" Bob Dylan sang. And within the Church this experience of change was shaped largely by ideology-driven pronouncements from theologians and journalists eager to declare, in "the spirit of Vatican II," that in the Church, like everywhere else, old ways were out and new ways were in.

• • •

The results are visible in numbers that depict the Catholic crisis in starkly empirical terms. Of course, numbers do not reach to the heart of religion, which is faith; but the numbers at least provide a general indication of what's been happening in American Catholicism in the last fifty to sixty years.

In considering these data points, keep in mind that they are for the country as a whole; the situation is significantly more complex from diocese to diocese. Generally speaking, and mirroring U.S. population shifts, the Church has been contracting in the old strongholds in the Northeast and Midwest, even as the Catholic population has risen sharply and continues to rise in the South and Southwest. That translates into big losses in old Catholic citadels like Boston, New York, and Chicago as well as Rust Belt cities, along with big increases in places like Houston, Dallas, Los Angeles, and San Diego.

Although the number of priests has been falling nationwide, at the same time some dioceses are experiencing a rise in priestly vocations, which is likely to continue. Even in those places, however, the supply of priests does not match the growth of Catholic population. So far as one can tell, Sunday Mass attendance has been declining for years in all parts of the country and is continuing to drop. (For obvious reasons, Mass attendance fell during COVID-induced lockdowns, but, as of this writing, attendance generally has not returned to pre-pandemic levels.) Sharp drops in Catholic marriages and infant baptisms also have occurred just about everywhere, but with variations in the rate of decline from diocese to diocese and region to region.

With that said, here are the numbers:[12]

- In 1970, there were 54.1 million Catholics in the United States; in 2019 (the last pre-pandemic year) there were 72.4 million. But even though the number of Catholics has gone up substantially, other indices are not encouraging. CARA doesn't provide a direct analysis of Catholic religiosity, but it does report that from 1970 to 2019, Catholics attending Mass weekly fell from 54.9% to 21.1%, even as those telling survey-takers that their religious affiliation was "strong" went from 45.8% to 32.2%.

- The number of Catholic priests in the United States in 1970 was 59,192 (37,272 diocesan, 21,920 religious order). By 2019, the total had dropped to 35,929 (24,857 diocesan, 11,072 religious). Priestly ordinations went from 805 in 1970 to 468 in 2019. Religious sisters numbered 160,931 in 1970 and 42,441 in 2019. Religious brothers went from 11,623 to 3,931. As might be expected, the median age among all three groups — priests, nuns, and brothers — shot up during these years and continues to rise. As this is written, fully a third of all U.S. priests are retired.

- In 1970, the 9,366 Catholic elementary schools enrolled 3.4 million students; in 2019, the 5,038 schools were attended by 1.2 million. At the secondary level, in 1970 there were 1,986 schools and 1.008 million students; in 2019, the 1,199 schools were attended by 555,901 students. Nor has non-school religious education taken up the slack. In 1970, there were 4.2 million primary-age and 1.3 million secondary-age students in parish religious education programs; in 2019, the numbers were 2.2 million primary-age and 527,344 secondary-age.

- Other statistics are also down. Infant baptisms —

1.089 million in 1970 — numbered only 582,331 in 2019. Catholic marriages — 426,309 in 1970 and 137,885 in 2019. Even Catholic funerals are down, dropping from 417,779 to 392, 277.[13]

Cardinal Gibbons saw American Catholicism blooming like a rose in his day, but no serious observer sees it that way now. Instead, as Ralph Martin, a leading figure in the Catholic Charismatic movement, remarks, in today's Church "Business as usual" means going "out of business."[14]

When will it end? *The New York Times* columnist Ross Douthat, a conservative Catholic, predicts that, rather than stabilizing as optimists might hope, the downward trend in American Catholicism will continue and even accelerate for the foreseeable future. Among the reasons, he cites "generational turnover" as devout older Catholics and "loosely affiliated Baby Boomer[s]" are replaced by children and grandchildren who are religiously "nonpracticing or nonaffiliated"; "continued fallout from the sex abuse crisis"; growing "institutional stress" as the number of priests continues to drop; falling Catholic immigration from Latin America; and "increasing hostility toward Catholicism, especially in more liberal states," resulting in the accelerated secularization of Catholic schools and hospitals.[15]

Bleak though Douthat's picture is, barring a miracle, it's almost certainly accurate. What does that imply for revitalizing the Church? How much can be saved? How much even should be saved? We are not going to waste time proposing strategies for reversing the irreversible and preventing the unpreventable. Rather, we hope to show how, looking at the situation realistically, Catholic lay people can help their Church weather this storm and emerge from it smaller, no doubt, but also — God willing — stronger.

• • •

To do that, though, we need to begin by taking a closer look at the decline of American Catholicism that has already occurred.

Earlier we pointed to secularization as the overarching explanation for the crisis of the churches, including the Catholic Church, in the United States and other Western countries. But although that is true in a broad sense, blaming "secularization" will not help much in deciding what the Catholic laity ought to do now. Simply saying, "Stop being secularized" is useless. Taking secularization as a given, we need a clear understanding of the specific factors contributing to the decline, for unless we understand how it happened, we are likely to end up battling shadows and prescribing remedies for imaginary ills.

Although the cultural turbulence of 1960s and 1970s provided the setting for much that happened in the Church, the downward trend actually began much earlier. In fact, it was taking shape in those seemingly golden years for American religion, the 1940s and 1950s. Here several contributing factors stand out.

One, following World War II, was the GI Bill and its promise of a free college education for military veterans. Make no mistake, the GI Bill was a great blessing that had enormously positive results. Many thousands of young Americans, including many Catholics, took advantage of this opportunity for advancement at government expense, often becoming the first members of their families to attend college, and in this way taking a giant step toward better jobs, higher incomes, and middle-class prosperity. As we shall see below, however, there also were unintended consequences.

A second factor was the great shift of population from cities to new, rapidly expanding suburbs. Until then, American Catholics were largely an urban people, living in city neighborhoods not uncommonly marked by a high degree of ethnic uniformity and focused on parishes that, in many cases, had been established specifically to serve particular nationality groups and offered a broad range of community-building religious devotions and social events. Now, however, upwardly mobile Catholics in growing numbers left these city enclaves and moved to the new suburbs where newly established parishes scrambled to serve widely dispersed, ethnically mixed populations of middle-class, college-educated Catholics who scarcely knew one another.

And then, as the children of these Catholics were reaching college age, the revolutionary 1960s exploded on the scene, uprooting settled beliefs and values. What before had seemed debauchery was treated as freedom and personal expression, adolescent arrogance became a sign of maturity, rejection of authority was saluted as heroic, abandoning formality and restraint was called "authentic," social utopianism became a kind of alternate religion and "truth" a matter of opinion.

In the Catholic sector, the deterioration in attachment to the Church that followed is often attributed to either or both of two notable events of the '60s: the Second Vatican Council and Pope St. Paul VI's encyclical *Humanae Vitae,* reaffirming the Church's condemnation of artificial contraception. But the stage had already been set by the failure — or inability — of Church institutions to offer sufficiently persuasive grounds for remaining attached to Catholicism in the face of serious inducements to disaffiliate. For where the old city parishes had largely succeeded in retaining the loyalty of immigrants and their children, the new suburban parishes with their attenuated sense of community struggled to do the same among college graduates and their offspring experiencing the opportunities and challenges of busy professional and social lives. How, one might ask, could Mass followed by coffee and donuts in the parish hall hope to compete with Sunday brunch at the country club?

As for attributing what happened to Vatican II and *Humanae Vitae,* sociologist Stephen Bullivant begs to differ. After all, virtually every other Christian body in the United States and

Great Britain has experienced the same hemorrhaging of practice, belief, and affiliation in the same time frame as the Catholic Church without having an ecumenical council and a birth control encyclical to blame. While "denomination-specific" factors like Vatican II and the encyclical may add "a bit of 'local color'" to the story of Catholic decline, he writes, they are "epiphenomenal to the general trends" — which is to say that, considered apart from a host of other factors, blaming Vatican II or *Humanae Vitae* or both just doesn't wash.[16]

Bullivant's own explanation focuses on the abrupt removal of plausibility structures that had previously kept British and American Catholics linked to Catholicism. For those unfamiliar with the expression, we note that *plausibility structure* is sociologists' term for a set of beliefs, attitudes, and behaviors, together with institutions and structures that embody and transmit them, that serve to maintain and reinforce a particular system of beliefs and values. Bullivant explains the undermining and collapse of Catholic plausibility structures this way:

> Our close-knit Catholic parishes, where one's neighbors, friends, workmates, and fellow parishioners were often coextensive, and in which one's social, ethnic, cultural, and sporting senses of community and belonging — as well as, of course, one's religious life — were often closely intertwined, are paradigmatic examples of such social 'deep architecture.' Though still seemingly going strong throughout much of the post-war period, the writing was already on the presbytery wall. The Second World War, among much else, lifted large numbers of young people out of these environments, before a slew of post-war social and economic changes … were already fracturing these semi-closed subcultures.[17]

Add to these forces a little later the further fracturing of Catholic plausibility structures by forces both external and internal to the Church. At the risk of repeating things already said, a partial list includes

- the cultural and sexual revolution of the 1960s
- the negative witness of thousands of defections from the priesthood and religious life
- the unsteady, and sometimes incoherent, introduction into parishes of innovations rightly or wrongly attributed to the ecumenical council, especially the abrupt and inadequately explained abandonment of hallowed forms of devotion, from scrapping the "fish on Friday" abstinence rule to relaxing the Eucharistic fast before communion
- the rise and toleration of institutionalized dissent within the Church that soon extended to much else besides birth control
- the systematic abandonment of old-line Catholic organizations and institutions in response to the urgings of Catholic intellectuals and opinion-leaders
- the encouragement of a shallow, one-religion-is-as-good-as-another brand of popular ecumenism.

And side by side with all this was the relentless advance of the cultural assimilation project that leaders like Gibbons and Ireland had blessed and promoted in their day, though now of course with results hugely different from those the Americanizers had foreseen.[18] Gibbons, Ireland, and the rest took for granted that Catholic assimilation, mediated by the plausibility structures of a healthy Catholic subculture, would be a benign process in which Catholics would remain faithful to the dogmas, morals, and worship of the Church even as they embraced the values of American culture and blended seamlessly into it. Now, though, the subculture was greatly weakened, while the plausibility structures of old had either been repudiated or set aside, with the Church offering little or nothing in their place.

As Bullivant remarks, the conventional wisdom of Catholic opinion leaders of the 1960s held that bringing the Church into fruitful dialogue with the modern world would require leveling the walls of the Catholic ghetto: "The Church and its practices would need to be less weird and culturally remote. ... Everything from the words of the Mass itself, to the dress habits of nuns, to the soft furnishings of confessionals, should be made more accessible and relevant." But the results were deeply disappointing. Instead of speaking old truths persuasively to modern ears, "Catholics 'became like everyone else' ... at precisely the moment as 'everybody else' started rapidly to become less orthodoxly believing, less regularly practicing, and ultimately, less religiously identifying."[19]

For the last fifty years, says Catholic author Robert Royal, "it seemed that almost anything was compatible with Catholicism," making it a matter of uncommon urgency that Catholics "recover the ancient wisdom that certain choices place you within the household, others outside."[20] Instead of increasing Catholic influence on secular culture and evangelizing it, however, assimilation — absent the identity-reinforcing support of healthy plausibility structures — has lessened the cultural impact of Catholicism. Says Archbishop Charles Chaput, retired archbishop of Philadelphia, the result of having been "outsiders" in America for so long was "a Catholic passion to fit in."[21] Assimilation accomplished that, and the results were unexpected. "That very success has weakened any chance the Church had to seize a 'Catholic moment' when Catholics might fill the moral hole in our culture created by the collapse of a Protestant consensus," writes Chaput.[22] As it is, the real surprise may not be that so little of traditional Catholicism has survived but, all things considered, so much — pointing perhaps to underlying, though largely unappreciated, strength and vitality in the tradition that holds significant hope for the future.

Be that as it may, though, polls repeatedly show large numbers of nominal Catholics holding views "just like everybody else" in support of things like abortion and same-sex marriage. An email account by a retired professor, a Catholic, concerning his experience of Catholic campus ministry at the university where he taught for years, sheds light on that: "They had little gatherings in a house owned by the parish. Six or seven students at most. They would simply cringe at the idea of presenting what the Church teaches for a campus audience. They would jump on the campaigns initiated by other groups emphasizing the ambiguous, secular causes of the day — tolerance, equality, all that. They didn't see that their message was that they had no message."[23]

Barring the radical change of conversion, Catholic lay people like those the professor describes will have little or nothing to contribute to revitalizing the Church. Surrounded by an aggressive, hostile secular culture, Catholics can ill afford to be just like everyone else if Catholicism is to survive as a significant presence in America.

But someone may object about the sex abuse scandal? Hasn't the horrendous reality of sexual abuse of minors by some priests, and its systematic cover-up by some bishops and religious superiors, played a major part in defections from the Church and rising suspicion of Catholicism among many non-Catholics? And doesn't it explain why even Catholics who have stuck with the Church aren't keen on getting behind her evangelization projects? Our Church's leaders have a long way to go to win back trust, and you can't blame that solely on the people you piously stigmatize as go-along-to-get-along Catholics.

The sex abuse scandal has done immeasurable harm, and the people overwhelmingly to blame for that are the perpetrators of abuse and the leaders who covered up their crimes. But granting that, fitting the sex abuse scandal into our calculus is not a simple, one-dimensional task. Bill Donohue, the redoubtable president of the Catholic League for Religious and Civil Rights, makes the important point that the scandal has been exploited by various groups — "the media, the entertainment industry, advocacy groups, victims' activists and their lawyers, state attorneys general, and others" — seeking, for reasons not in all cases admirable, to embarrass and damage the Church. At the same time, however, Donohue readily acknowledges — as any rational and decent person must do — that the guilty priests and negligent bishops and superiors responsible for this disaster have done an enormous disservice to the Church as well as enormous injury to abuse victims.[24]

And the toxic effects linger on. One whole subset of problems concerns the fact that many American dioceses are now strapped for cash — and not a few have gone into bankruptcy — as a result of paying out enormous sums in settlements. As to the role of abuse in encouraging defections from the Church, Bullivant suggests the scandal "acts as one (more) reason — and an evidently weighty one — for not thinking of oneself as a Catholic. ... This effect would not, necessarily, come on suddenly and strongly, since such people typically have only a weak attachment to the Church. However, both the constant 'drip-drip' of negative stories, and the concomitant tainting of the 'Catholic brand' within the wider culture, exert an influence."[25] And this unquestionably has led some Catholics to decide that, rather than lend a helping hand, they will happily let "the Church" — the institutional, hierarchical Church, that is — stew in her own juice.

• • •

Many conclusions can be drawn from all this, but the overriding conclusion we draw is that the Catholic Church in the United States is at a tipping point. What comes next — continued decline to the point of social, cultural, and political irrelevance or, just possibly, some version of a fresh start?

Whatever a fresh start for the Church might look like, it must begin in faith — not just faith of any sort either, but faith of a special kind. "Christian faith," as the philosopher-theologian Germain Grisez points out, is "a personal faith in Jesus, an immediate relationship with him." Faith like this, he explains, "really does unite Christians immediately with Jesus because in making it they enter into the covenant community, the Church, in which he is personally present."[26] This more than anything else justifies us in having confidence in the Church's future.

In a radio interview in 1969, theologian Joseph Ratzinger — the future Pope Benedict XVI — was asked, "What will become of the Church in the future?" His answer, often quoted since then, is a remarkably prescient description of what the Church in the United States has experienced in the years since then and is experiencing now, as well as a faith-filled vision of what the Church may yet become:

> From the crisis of today the Church of tomorrow will emerge — a Church that has lost much. She will become small and will have to start afresh more or less from the beginning. She will no longer be able to inhabit many of the edifices built in prosperity. As the number of her adherents diminishes, so will she lose many of her social privileges. ...
>
> The Church will be a more spiritual Church, not presuming upon a political mandate, flirting as little with the Left as with the Right. It will be hard going for the Church, for the process of crystallization and clarification will cost her much valuable energy. It will make

her poor and cause her to become the Church of the meek. The process will be all the more arduous, for sectarian narrow-mindedness as well as pompous self-will will have to be shed. … But when the trial of this sifting is past, a great power will flow from a more spiritualized and simplified Church. Men in a totally planned world will find themselves unspeakably lonely. If they have completely lost sight of God, they will feel the whole horror of their poverty. Then they will discover the little flock of believers as something wholly new. They will discover it as a hope that is meant for them, an answer for which they have always been searching in secret.[27]

Next we shall begin to consider what Catholic lay people can and must do in order to contribute responsibly to the long, painful, and, in the end, richly fulfilling process of "sifting" from which, we must pray, the Church will emerge more spiritualized and simplified than it has been since perhaps the very earliest centuries of Christianity.

— 3 —

Three Versions
of the Future

Toward a New Subculture

It's been said the "C" in Christian and Catholic "has become the new scarlet letter,"[1] marking its bearers for shaming, social ostracism, and a witches' brew of personal and collective penalties adding up to persecution. Citing Nathaniel Hawthorne's classic tale of Puritanism and guilt may be a bit of a stretch, but it does make an important point. As author Mary Eberstadt explains, the pressing question for many Christians, including not a few

Catholics, is fast becoming not how to resist the rising tide of hostile secularism but, "Where will we go?" Declaring the situation "like nothing that has happened before," Eberstadt believes the options for Western religious believers boil down to withdrawing into semi-monastic communities or "stand[ing] tall as witnesses" to faith against the onslaught of unbelief.[2]

Reading this, people of Irish heritage might object that, far from being unprecedented, something resembling the state of affairs described by writers like Eberstadt and Rod Dreher befell their forebears in Ireland in the seventeenth and eighteenth centuries. Other nationalities and ethnic groups, including Black Americans and American Indians, might point to their own victimization. And Jews might say with justice that pogroms and other forms of persecution — including the Holocaust — are part of Jewish history. The mistreatment of disfavored groups truly is a familiar story with many different chapters.

Still, the Dreher-Eberstadt thesis underlines an important fact about what may now await faithful Christians at the hands of intolerant elites in the secularized West, including the United States. Except for the abuse of Blacks and Indians, there is little if anything in American history to compare with the outpouring of hostility and contempt lately directed at Catholics and other Christians by Hollywood, major news organizations, and even secular academic institutions. Now, prominent people in public life, the media, and entertainment appear to have drawn the conclusion that for them the path to getting ahead lies in not only repudiating traditional values on abortion and marriage but also trashing those who hold them.

Eberstadt and others trace the ultimate source of all this to the sexual revolution. As "the centerpiece of a new orthodoxy and new morality," she writes, the revolution in thinking and behavior in regard to sex goes a long way to explain "the outsize hostility toward believers who have been minding their own business, or trying to educate their children, or expressing their faith in public forums — or otherwise behaving in ways that once invited no penalties, and now do."[3]

Understanding how we got into our present fix thus requires examining the sources of the revolution in sexual morality.

The ideological background of this and other assaults on traditional ideas of right and wrong undoubtedly can be found in the influence of philosophical relativism — the systematic rejection of the idea that there is any such thing as absolute, unchangeable truth (with the idea that there is no such thing as absolute truth as the sole exception). This, however, is radically incompatible with a belief system like Catholicism, founded as it is on the truth of Divine Revelation. Nonessential elements of Catholic belief and practice can and do change, but a faithful Catholic doesn't have the option of denying a statement like "Sexual activity outside the marriage of a man and woman is sinful" or even responding, "It depends on the circumstances."

Prominent in the history of the sexual revolution are such names as Sigmund Freud, Wilhelm Reich, Havelock Ellis, Margaret Sanger, and Alfred Kinsey.[4] Two events of particular importance in its development and promotion were the appearance in English of Reich's book (first published in German in 1936) *The Sexual Revolution,* and the 1948 publication of Kinsey's *Sexual Behavior in the Human Male.* These writers understood quite well what they were doing and what they hoped to bring about. A student of these matters says of Reich, "His initial thesis that sexual processes were always the nucleus of cultural processes in society meant that reorganizing the patterns of sexual life would eventually lead to a social revolution. In other words, eroticization was viewed as an excellent tool to destroy all relationships based on authority, which in turn could be used to rebuild the entire social structure."[5]

Wrapped in the cultural fog of relativism and utilitarianism, the deconstruction of sexual morality made rapid progress. The first serious break in the ranks of churches that up to then had opposed contraception occurred in 1930, when the Anglicans' Lambeth Conference gave limited approval to the use of contraceptives by married couples. Pope Pius XI responded later that year with a strongly-worded condemnation of artificial birth control in his encyclical on Christian marriage *Casti Connubii*, but by then it was common knowledge that many Catholic couples were practicing contraception.[6]

Even so, Catholic teaching on contraception remained unchallenged, though not universally observed, by Catholics until the 1960s. Then, in the midst of cultural revolution, the expectation of change in the Church's position on birth control spread rapidly among Catholics. It was encouraged and given an appearance of legitimacy by some theologians and media as well as by leaks from the papal "birth control commission" — a body originally established by Pope St. John XXIII to consider the Church's position on population questions — that by now had become deeply involved in re-evaluating Catholic teaching on oral contraception. In this way the stage was set for the angry, organized public dissent that greeted Pope St. Paul VI's 1968 encyclical *Humanae Vitae* reaffirming the Church's established doctrine on contraception.

Since then, fresh pressure to surrender to the sexual revolution has been brought to bear on the Church by the legalization of abortion and same-sex marriage, together with the increasingly aggressive campaign on behalf of LGBTQ interests. As this is written, familiar secular drums are now being beaten on behalf of legal recognition of polyamory — intimate relationships among three (or more) persons — as a legitimate form of marriage. At each stage along the way, the Church has been berated for holding supposedly reactionary views on sex, with some Catholic opinion leaders joining the chorus and calling on the

Church to fall in step with the times.

• • •

So, to the list of factors examined in the previous chapter that, operating at first from outside the Church and more recently from within, help to account for the present crisis in American Catholicism, let us by all means add the sexual revolution. And here's the bottom line: Turmoil within the Church, mirroring turmoil in the wider society, destroyed the unity in belief and practice that had long existed within the Catholic subculture. Against this dispiriting background, three — and *only* three — versions of the immediate future are realistic possibilities for the Catholic Church in America. Let's take a look at each.

VERSION NUMBER ONE
Continuing decline, with eventual stabilization at some unknown point in the future.
It's tempting to call this the *que sera, sera* scenario, but charity dictates that it be designated "responsible management of an institution in decline." Whatever name it might be given, it corresponds to Ralph Martin's remark that "Business as usual" for the Church these days means going "out of business."[7] Its working assumption is that an irreversible institutional and numerical decline of American Catholicism will continue for the foreseeable future — as almost certainly *will* happen — and that the role of Church leaders in such circumstances is mainly to manage the closings and the cutbacks responsibly.

And in fact this can already be seen happening in the growing number of dioceses where bishops, responding to a shortage of clergy and declining lay participation in the Church, are anxious to keep providing sacramental services to as many people as possible. Consistent with the limitations of a religious body in irreversible decline, these bishops have begun closing arguably superfluous parishes entirely or else consolidating them into larger parochial units.

These numbers for the Church in the United States from the Center for Applied Research in the Apostolate (CARA) suggest what's been happening.[8]

- Number of parishes: 18,224 in 1970 and 16,914 in 2019
- Active diocesan priests per parish: 1.8 in 1970 and 1.0 in 2019
- Parishes without a resident priest pastor: 571 in 1970 and 3,572 in 2019
- Parishes where the bishop has turned over pastoral care to a deacon or other non-priest: 7 in 1975 (no number given for 1970) and 378 in 2019[9]

At its best, the reaction to numbers like these is mildly hopeful resignation — as in this remark by Cardinal Wilton Gregory of Washington, a prelate who has watched this situation taking shape during his four decades as a member of the hierarchy: "We are often impatient people calling for immediate answers. If it took a generation or more to come to this state of affairs, it will probably take at least that long to chart a better future."[10]

He may be right. But in a number of places in the United States, the Church already has been coping with a clergy shortage for years and has experienced some success in doing so. In 1978, one of the present authors was at that time a lay employee of the Glenmary Home Missioners and published a book describing the emergence in some places of "regional parishes" in which several priests lived together in a central location and served all of the communities in their particular county.[11] Since then there have been other, similar experiments in a number of dioceses, some driven by simple necessity and others by a search for effective pastoral solutions.

As more dioceses move in this direction, there are realistic grounds for hoping the local churches will find ways to adjust. The Church in mission territory USA — Appalachia, parts of the Deep South and Southwest, the Rocky Mountain states, and American dependencies from Puerto Rico to Guam — unquestionably needs help from the worldwide Church in the form of personnel, but up to now the structures and ministries in place are, for the most part, holding up well.

True, no one really knows what to expect as similar conditions spread from areas that traditionally have been American Catholicism's "home missions" to the rest of the country. But if the good Lord wills it, the promised land, following some years of responsibly managed decline, might be stabilized. If so, however, this probably will be stabilization as a remnant religious body, far smaller in numbers and influence than the Church that most urban and suburban Catholics grew up in and still take for granted — a "Church that has lost much" as predicted by Joseph Ratzinger in the prophetic utterance quoted in chapter 2.

And that is no cause for celebration. For in this scenario, the American Church will have a dismaying resemblance to the Church as it now exists in some predominantly Muslim countries and, more and more, in the highly secularized nations of Western Europe: faithful believers who make up a barely tolerated minority, struggling to survive in a hostile environment and having little or no political or cultural weight.[12] Contemplating the prospect of a future like our Version Number One, Mary Eberstadt says, "What many Western men and women of faith feel to the marrow these days is fear."[13]

VERSION NUMBER TWO
The Benedictine Solution and the Community of Disciples

Back in the winter of 1947 — just after World War II, that is — Romano Guardini delivered a set of lectures at Germany's Tubingen University that later became a small book with the English title *The End of the Modern World*. Monsignor Guardini was a distinguished theologian of the years preceding the Second Vatican Council, and his reflections were those of a deeply spiritual and scholarly man reacting to the horrors of the recently ended war. But his analysis of the human situation as he found it then is, if anything, still more timely now.

> Man is being given ever more power of decision and control over world reality, but man himself is removing himself farther and farther from the norms which spring from the truth of being and from the demands of goodness and holiness.[14] Contemporary man can bring himself to destruction of both the interior and exterior orders or he can fashion a new universal order, a space where he could fit himself and, conscious of human dignity, lay the roadway for the future.[15]

So far, the first option of destruction appears on its way to being realized in the United States and countries like it. The great question for American Catholics and other believers now is where to find space for survival and renewal at a time when the antihuman dark forces of falsehood and immorality appear to be dictating the course of events.

This is the state of affairs prompting journalist and author Rod Dreher's widely discussed proposal that religious believers adopt what he memorably called "the Benedict Option." The name refers to St. Benedict of Nursia, who in the dark days of the sixth century, amid the rubble of the collapsed Roman Empire, became the founder of the Western monasticism that managed to keep the Christian intellectual and spiritual fire alive against the encroaching darkness of barbarism.

Taking philosopher Alasdair MacIntyre as his inspiration, and citing the Supreme Court's 2015 *Obergefell* decision declaring a constitutional right to same-sex marriage as the final defeat of traditional values in the culture war ("the Waterloo of religious conservatism"[16]), Dreher explained the Benedict Option this way:

> The idea is that serious Christian conservatives could no longer live business-as-usual lives in America, that we have to develop creative, communal solutions to help us hold onto our faith and our values in a world growing ever more hostile to them. We would have to choose to make a decisive leap into a truly countercultural way of living Christianity, or we would doom our children and our children's children to assimilation.[17]

With the decadence of contemporary secular culture taken as a starting point, Dreher made a vigorous case that Christian conservatives — among whom he included traditional Catholics — had to organize themselves in small communities of the like-minded ("Benedict Option communities") to preserve and celebrate traditional values and beliefs, to provide reinforcement and encouragement to one another, and to collaborate in transmitting the faith to their children.

Contrary to what some of his critics imagine, Dreher did not advocate literal, physical withdrawal from secular America — he wasn't issuing a "take to the hills" solution. Rather, he prescribed a process in which believers consciously set themselves intellectually, affectively, and spiritually apart for the sake of preserving deeply cherished beliefs. "These communities start with the individual heart and spread from there to the family, the church community, the neighborhood," he wrote.[18]

This is hardly new. Saint Paul told his Corinthian converts to avoid contact with "the immoral of this world," explaining that what he had in mind was not physical withdrawal from society but shunning Eucharistic fellowship with a persistent public sinner (see 1 Cor 5: 9–11). The continuing debate among Catholics over whether to give Communion to Catholic politicians who support abortion echoes this episode from Christianity's early days and raises much the same questions.

Dreher's Benedict Option is not the only proposal of its kind. Another, advanced by Cardinal Avery Dulles, SJ, can be found in the 2002 expanded edition of his influential 1974 study *Models of the Church*. Even faithful Catholics, Dulles wrote, "rarely experience Church as a community of mutual support and stimulation. ... They find it hard to relate the Church to their daily life, which is lived out in a very secular environment. When religion is so divorced from daily life, it begins to appear peripheral and even unreal."[19] As an antidote, Dulles proposed the creation of "communities in which people can experience a full Christian environment," which he described as "something analogous to the religious novitiate." These "noviates for life," he said, would serve as "training grounds for lay leaders in the community of disciples."[20]

Dulles's proposal clearly reflects his own experience of formation as a young member of the Society of Jesus. Unfortunately, the use of the term "noviates" to describe what he had in mind has a clericalist ring that's likely to be off-putting for many lay Catholics. It also looks (at first sight, at least) like an elitist plan for preparing a small body of future leaders rather than forming the mass of believers. But even so, the idea deserves to be taken seriously. Training future lay leaders is important, as the Catholic Action movement of years past realistically recognized, and by no means is there enough of it today.

In tandem with Dreher's analysis, Dulles' proposal shows that intelligent, concerned observers are seeking ways to respond to the secular culture's negative impact on faith. And they see the absence of community and continuing formation in the religious experience of so many believers as serious deficiencies calling for radical countermeasures.

VERSION NUMBER THREE
New Communities for a New Subculture

When *The Benedict Option* appeared in 2017, Rod Dreher's clarion call to religious Americans was widely hailed for its analysis of the secularist assault on faith and its prophetic vision of a survival strategy for the faithful. "The most discussed and most important religious book of the decade," *New York Times* columnist David Brooks enthused in a blurb.[21]

But others had doubts. One of them is political scientist Susan Orr Traffas, a professor at Benedictine College in Atchison, Kansas, who in a paper presented to the Fellowship of Catholic Scholars complained that what she took to be Dreher's call for Christians to opt out of political life "goes against Christ's call to go out into the world." Christians, she said, "are not called to be as the Amish, withdrawn from the world. We are to be a proselytizing people. This is a function that we cannot perform if we are in a community only of those who already agree with us. Wouldn't that at least be a failure of charity? Aren't those who live in spiritual poverty today to be included in the 'least of these' as much as the physically poor?"[22]

There is also the matter of practicality. In his history of Plymouth Plantation, Governor William Bradford laments that the Pilgrims' church, founded by people who had come to the New World seeking liberty to practice their version of faith freely, began to fragment within twenty years. Today, surely, an aggressively secularist culture could ignore free-standing Benedict-style communities outside traditional ecclesiastical structures until they collapsed or simply faded away.[23]

But, someone might say, now there is hope on the horizon — a powerful defender of religion against the inroads of aggressive secularism in the somewhat surprising form of the United States Supreme Court. And, true enough, the court, with a six-member conservative majority at the time this is written, has lately been more friendly to religious liberty claims than it had been for many years. But while this is a welcome development, who can say how long it will last, given the shifting tides of politics and Supreme Court nominations? And even in the best of circumstances, the Supreme Court cannot single-handedly repel the secularist onslaught but can only mitigate the damage in the realm of constitutional jurisprudence. Meanwhile, the rabid hostility of the mainstream secularist media reacting to the court's recent shift makes the nature of the present crisis still more obvious while reinforcing the need for religious groups to devise and implement their own strategies of resistance.

In the Catholic sector of the religious world, the laity have the potential for countering secularist hostility on a broad front. Among events of the past that illustrate that point, the development of the Catholic school system stands out. The Third Plenary Council of Baltimore's mandate to create a Catholic school system was a bold assertion of Catholic identity, a refusal to expose Catholic children to Protestant-tinged public schooling. And the lay people of that day, convinced that their Catholic faith and practice were worth preserving, responded by creating a remarkable educational system that survived and thrived for more than a century.

Now, along with much else, saving the Church calls for comparable grit and determination in saving a Catholic school system that has shrunk drastically in the last sixty-five years. At the same time, it requires fresh creativity and commitment in accepting the challenge to adopt new ways of transmitting the faith to the younger generation, especially by motivating and training Catholic parents as primary educators of their children (more on that below).

Susan Orr Traffas makes the point that Catholics are supposed to be "proselytizing people."[24] Although the negative connotations of "proselytizing" make it preferable to speak of "evangelizing," we agree heartily with the fundamental point. We know from experience how difficult it is to make a commitment to evangelization part of the everyday practice of an average parish, but the need has never been greater than it is now. Since evangelization is not an optional add-on but an essential part of what the Church is — a community of believers sent into the world to preach the Gospel — it has to be a constitutive part of any Catholic survival strategy. Such a strategy must combine Dreher's emphasis on affective, intellectual, and spiritual separation from the corrupt secular culture with the evangelizing imperative that is an inseparable element of Catholic identity.

Easier said than done, of course. But useful indicators for getting started do exist.

Avery Dulles makes a strong case for a model of the Church that, borrowing a phrase from Pope St. John Paul II, he calls a "community of disciples." This, he argues, was the form the Church had in the early centuries when being a Catholic "retained something of that demanding and heroic character evident in the New Testament concept of discipleship."

> The Christian community continued to be a contrast society, maintaining a certain critical distance from its pagan environment. Frequently, it would appear, the faithful were required or at least strongly exhorted to abstain

from engaging in war, from frequenting the baths and stadiums, and from wearing wigs and jewelry. Among themselves they practiced intense mutual love, caring for the poor and the sick, the widows and orphans, and extending hospitality to travelers. ... Conscious of the demands of discipleship, the faithful were prepared for imprisonment, exile, and even death.[25]

Understanding the Church as a community of disciples and acting accordingly, Dulles holds, is particularly timely today, when the Church once more faces a secularist culture wielding powerful tools of persuasion and coercion. It is also particularly well suited to the Catholic laity's vocation to evangelize, as Dulles explains:

The laity, in fact, have special responsibility to penetrate the secular sphere with the spirit of Christ, and to leaven it with the yeast of the gospel, so that human efforts may be sustained by hope and guided toward the divinely appointed consummation. In our day the challenges of marriage and parenthood are enormous, as are the problems of introducing Christian norms into the worlds of business, government, and the professions. Only the committed disciple can measure up to these challenges.[26]

The emergence in modern times of new, largely lay groups — Communion and Liberation, Opus Dei, the Neocatechumenal Way, and others — reflects growing recognition of the importance of lay discipleship.

One might object that, while what Dulles and others like him say is fine for people in leadership positions — the CEO, the department chair, the boss — it makes impossible demands on ordinary individuals. These average people either do their jobs according to policies and rules set by others higher up in their organizations or else labor in humble fields of endeavor, useful in their own way but with little or no significant impact on the course of society and the world.

That's a good point. And it has a good answer. The current situation and the challenge it presents resemble the situation and challenge around the year AD 200. In a document that has come down to us as the Epistle to Diognetus, an anonymous Christian apologist said this of his fellow Christians: "While they dwell in both Greek and non-Greek cities, as each one's lot was cast, and conform to the customs of the country in dress, food, and mode of life in general, the whole tenor of their way of living stamps it as worthy of admiration and admittedly extraordinary. ... What the soul is in the body, that the Christians are in the world."[27]

It hardly needs saying that today's world is very different from the world of AD 200, and yet the challenge and opportunity for the laity remain much the same, as St. Josemaría Escrivá, founder of the lay organization Opus Dei, illustrates:

> God is calling you to serve him in and from the ordinary, secular and civil activities of human life. He waits for us every day, in the laboratory, in the operating theatre, in the army barracks, in the university chair, in the factory, in the workshop, in the fields, in the home, and in all the immense panorama of work. ...
>
> [This consideration] should lead you to do your work perfectly, to love God and your fellowmen by putting love in the little things of everyday life, and discovering that divine something which is hidden in small details.[28]

That doesn't solve all difficulties, but it's a reminder that the difficulties are no excuse for not trying.

We shall say more in the next chapter about the need for the laity to engage in apostolate and do evangelization. For now, we simply repeat a point already made: Given the serious obstacles to realizing and sustaining this vision of the laity's role in today's world, a reconstituted Catholic subculture with a revitalized network of plausibility structures is desperately needed. As an environment of the spirit, this new subculture needs to exist within yet significantly apart from the secular culture; embrace distinctively Catholic beliefs, values, and ways of acting; be organized around authentically Catholic institutions, groups, and movements; and function largely, though not exclusively, within the canonical and pastoral forms of diocese and parish.

The old Catholic subculture that once existed is gone for good. But here and there a new Catholic subculture is emerging, with new educational institutions, new media ventures, new organizations and movements of many kinds. Let's hope and pray these prove capable of nurturing and sustaining the community of disciples the Catholic Church in America must become to regain her former vitality.

Central to this hoped-for resurgence is the parish, the heart of the Church's presence everywhere. Parishes and dioceses need to reorganize and reorient themselves in ways that take realistic account of the Church's weakened position. Since there will be fewer priests in the foreseeable future, deacons, religious women (also in sharp numerical decline, however), and lay people will be called on to administer parishes and perform defined pastoral roles more and more. But bishops must not make the disastrous mistake of lowering standards of competence and orthodoxy simply to fill otherwise vacant slots. Better to face the future short-handed than surrender the reins to unsuitable leadership.

Parishes themselves will be fewer in number and in many places will be grouped in parochial "clusters" covering relatively large geographical areas — no longer a parish every few blocks in the cities, no longer a parish in every county in much of rural America where the Church already has mission status.

Most important of all, what parishes are for will need rethinking, and this will require the collaboration of clergy and laity under episcopal guidance. High priority should go to creating — or encouraging, where they already exist — small groups of lay people who gather regularly in homes for prayer, mutual support, and assistance to neighbors in need. These should include, but not be limited to, prayer groups, reading and discussion groups (reading and discussing solid Catholic titles that is, not just the current best-sellers), support groups of various kinds, and groups for married couples and parents, including single parents. Old line organizations like the Knights of Columbus should be a welcome part of the mix along with new trans-parochial groups and movements that promote lay apostolate, evangelization, and social action.

• • •

Especially, the new Catholic subculture will have to address the growing crisis of transmitting the faith — or, more accurately, failing to transmit it — to children and young people.

Ads for Catholic schools and educational programs typically feature photos of attractive, bright-eyed kids who appear to be enthusiastically involved in the formation they're receiving. Would that these children were typical! But they aren't. Large numbers of American Catholic children and young people now receive little or no formation in the Faith, with the predictable result of ignorance of what the Church teaches and carelessness in religious practice — supposing these kids practice at all, as many do not.

Reflecting on the causes of Catholic disaffiliation, Stephen Bullivant laconically remarks that the faith formation of many

Catholics today is "very weak or nominal."[29] More often than not, parental negligence is at the root of the problem. That isn't true only of parents who are short on money and time to devote to their kids' religious formation. Frequently, parents who send their offspring to expensive private schools and summer camps, pay for their lessons in music and sports, and treat them to the culture-broadening experience of foreign travel nevertheless make little or no provision for their religious formation beyond the minimum required by the Church as a condition for receiving confirmation — the sacrament itself not uncommonly viewed as a social event more than an important stage in a young person's faith life.

Parental negligence is documented and analyzed by sociologists Christian Smith of Notre Dame and Amy Adamczyk of the John Jay College of Criminal Justice and the City University of New York in their book *Handing Down the Faith*. Their most important finding: "Above and beyond any other effect on children's religion is the influence of their parents. Rarely do or can other factors — congregations, youth groups, religious schools, mission or service trips — override the formative power of parents. The more aware and intentional religious parents are about this, the more effectively they should be able to shape their children religiously."[30]

Since the Church has repeatedly stressed that primacy of the parental role in education, this should be no surprise to Catholics. And yet, hasn't the point often been made by churchmen as they simultaneously pressed parents to do their duty by turning their children over to ecclesiastical institutions — Catholic schools and religious education programs — for formation in the faith? Nothing wrong with that, of course; but first things really should come first, and time and again these same churchmen did little or nothing to educate and motivate Catholic parents in their role as the most important agents of handing on the faith. "Give us a boy, and we'll give you back a man" used to be the motto of those famous educators, the Jesuits. But perhaps a better message to Catholic parents would be "Allow us to lend you a hand in carrying out your duty to raise your daughter or son as a person of deep faith and committed discipleship."

Plainly, though, many Catholic parents have neither received such a message, nor heeded it if they have. The Culture of American Families Survey, cited by Smith and Adamczyk, found that only a dismaying 17% of Catholic parents considered it "very important or essential" that their children share their faith. (The figure for mainline Protestants also was 17%, while for Jewish parents it was 13% and for Unitarians — 0%. But among conservative Protestants the figure rose to 48% and among Black Protestants to 58%.)[31] Another set of figures Smith and Adamcyzk provide from Faith and Family in America sheds light on the influence that parents exert — or fail to exert — on children's religious decisions. Among Catholics, 63% agreed "strongly" or "somewhat" that children should choose a religion — or *no* religion, for that matter — entirely on their own, with only 37% saying parents should encourage their offspring to accept their parents' faith.[32]

Smith and Adamczyk are social scientists, not counselors, but near the end of their book they offer two modest suggestions.

One is that, along with practicing the faith themselves, parents should talk to their children about it. "If there were only one practical take-away from our research," they write, "it would be this: parents need not only to 'walk the walk' but also regularly to *talk* with their children about their walk, what it means, why it matters, why they care." The second suggestion is that parents practice what the authors call a "general authoritative" style when it comes to parenting. "Combining clear and implemented life standards and expectations for their children with expressive emotional warmth and relational bonding … fosters relationships that most enhance effective religious transmission," they write.[33]

That is excellent advice. Parents fret about children's sports performance, vaccines, college choices, and much else. Many professed Catholics need similar stirrings of parental responsibility when it comes to handing on the Faith.

• • •

Besides a strong emphasis on the role of parents in faith formation, several other initiatives under the broad heading of "education" should be prominent elements of the new Catholic subculture.

One of these — an obvious, meritorious expression of parental right and responsibility — is homeschooling, no longer a fringe activity for an exceptional handful but a growing enterprise said to be educating an impressive 2.5 million American children as of 2019.[34] That homeschooling parents don't conform to the stereotypical image of a fringe group is clear from the finding that about two-thirds of the fathers and nearly as many of the mothers have bachelor's degrees or better while the median income of homeschooling families is well above average. Homeschoolers tend to be bright, savvy people who know what they're doing and do it because they judge it to be best for their children.

Which, come to think of it, probably explains why homeschooling is often attacked by hatchet men — and women — of the woke secularist culture, always alert to defame and quash non-conformity to right thinking as they define it while imposing a de facto public school monopoly on the education of the vast majority of children.

Considering the forces lined up against them, why do some parents choose homeschooling? The reasons, several of them likely to be operative for many parents, include reinforcing parent-child bonding, providing for children with special aptitudes and needs that may not get much attention in ordinary schools, shielding kids from perverse currents of thought — transgenderism and critical race theory are current examples — now infiltrating public education, and, perhaps most important of all, transmitting the beliefs and values of a religious tradition.

This concern and the opposition to it are hardly new. The parental right was overwhelmingly affirmed in 1925 by the Supreme Court's decision in the celebrated Oregon School Case. Striking down a crude attempt to destroy parochial schools by requiring all children to attend public schools, the court delivered a broad declaration of the fundamental right of parents, protected by the due process clause of the Fourteenth Amendment, to "direct the upbringing and education of children under their control." A child, the court said, "is not the mere creature of the State; those who nurture him and direct his destiny have the right, coupled with the high duty, to recognize and prepare him for additional obligations."[35] Yet what then seemed obvious to a unanimous court whose members included Oliver Wendell Holmes, Jr. and Louis Brandeis is today under attack by secular intellectuals who question the right of competent parents to school their own children.

Beyond homeschooling, the new Catholic subculture will also include schools themselves, both traditional Catholic elementary and secondary schools that survive the present weeding-out process and a goodly number of the new "classical academies" that *First Things* editor R. R. Reno predicts will have "significant influence in the years to come." Having begun in reaction against educational mediocrity, he writes, the academies are now expressions of a deliberate rejection of "wokery" in general and in some cases of "theologized versions of progressive ideology" that have found their way into some established

Catholic schools. Parents and educators responsible for classical academies "are doing something of incalculable importance, not just for the students under their care, but for the Church and our society," Reno says.[36]

The distinctive character of these institutions can be seen in the curriculum of the St. Jerome Institute, a Catholic classical academy in the Washington, DC, suburb of Hyattsville, Maryland. It includes seminars in humanities, art history, natural philosophy, and mathematics, organizes its third-year program around reflection on the nature and destiny of the human person, and, along with other subjects, teaches Latin, described as being "crucial ... for unlocking the treasures of our Western heritage."

Two national organizations now provide support for classical academies and offer information for interested inquirers: the Institute for Catholic Liberal Education, for specifically Catholic academies, and the Association of Classical Christian Schools, for largely Protestant ones. Says one writer: "Both the ACCS and ICLE comfortably deploy a vocabulary of 'the revival of learning' which has to do with both the souls of students and the culture of America. Though both consider themselves to be outside the mainstream — indeed, countercultural — they nevertheless maintain a civic-minded attitude toward their communities, and a commitment to helping American culture revive through traditional notions about wisdom, virtue, truth, goodness, and beauty."[37]

The formation of the young in the Catholic subculture must, of course, extend beyond the secondary level to include colleges and universities with a strong, visible commitment to their Catholic identity. Some already existing schools meet this description, and one can only hope they grow and thrive even as new ones join their ranks. Equally necessary, and deserving of support, are Catholic media enterprises that combine orthodoxy with professional excellence, including publishers of books and periodicals and producers of films, television programming, audiovisuals, and digital media content.

The point isn't that Catholics should read only approved Catholic books, watch only Catholic TV, etc. While a cautious approach to secular media really is necessary at a time when many are mouthpieces for secularist values and, in some cases, actively hostile to religion, people of faith nevertheless can and should make selective, discriminating use of them. And, looking at media as a field for apostolate, a broadly Christian presence there is badly needed, and talented Christian communicators should seek opportunities for breakthroughs into media now largely closed against them.

This is a reminder that the new subculture mustn't be closed in on itself, celebrating lost glories of the Catholic past and deploring excesses of the secularist present. The Church will need to make continuing, creative use of the Internet and social media as tools of evangelization and formation of all kinds and at all levels. A worthy project would be a practical handbook showing geographically-dispersed parochial clusters how to create and operate their own media-based interactive networks. A parish home page on the internet is a good first step, but the potential for catechesis, prayer, and other activities goes far beyond that.

Today, of course, many good people are rightly concerned about the harm social media do to children and young people. The injuries range upward in seriousness, from being a distraction and eating up time better spent on something else, to isolating young users from healthy social interaction with peers, increasing loneliness, providing easy access to pornography and perversion, opening the door to electronic bullying and sexual exploitation, and fostering suicidal thoughts and actual suicides.[38]

But given the universal presence of the new media in modern life — and especially in the lives of young people — it would be hopelessly unrealistic, as well as an opportunity lost, for the Church simply to shake her head in disapproval and walk away from them. Yet even now many churchmen still apparently believe they are communicating with people by issuing long, unreadable documents. Print media still have an important place in the total spectrum of modern communication (we wouldn't be writing this book otherwise), and that will continue for a long time. But it's only one place among many. Calling the Internet "the greatest invention in the field of communication since the printing press," Bishop Robert Barron, a diligent and effective evangelizer via new media, says, "If the Church does not get into that world, it would be a great mistake."[39]

Besides using media for evangelization, the most important thing the Church of the new subculture can do in relation to media may be to provide young Catholics (and not only the young) with formation in their use. Fr. Paul Soukup, SJ, a professor of communications at Santa Clara University, argues that to help students reflect on their faith tradition, religious educators must "first ... teach something of the tradition, the process of reflection, the need to think, and the need to evaluate materials available to them," including the multitude of "materials," good and bad, available in the digital world where so many spend so much of their time today.[40]

· · ·

As this sketch of a vision for the future of American Catholicism makes clear, the future won't be easy. But who said it would? We turn next to specific things lay people must do if the years of transition that lie ahead aren't to be a long, painful slog of decline and dissolution but an era of faith-filled creativity and hope.

— 4 —

Building a Cathedral

A Program for Saving the Church

People have marveled for centuries at the soaring magnificence of Cologne Cathedral's twin spires, the other-worldly beauty of Chartres Cathedral's stained glass, the multiple splendors of other cathedrals that grace Europe's landscape like hymns in stone, testifying in an age of disbelief to the inspired vision of those who built them in the Age of Faith.

Who were those builders? At a time when selfies, tweets, Facebook pages, and compulsive self-promotion are all the rage, when individuals hungering after instant celebrity unblushingly display their aberrations to a jaundiced public in TV interviews and social media, the people who built the cathedrals remain stubbornly anonymous. All we know for certain is that small armies of architects, builders, masons, artisans, sculptors, and fabricators of stained glass labored for many years to create these inspiring testimonials to transcendence.

Now it's time for American Catholics to do some cathedral building of our own. Which is to say: Without expecting or even wanting recognition or thanks, each of us needs to take responsibility for her or his share in the great project of revitalizing the Catholic Church in the United States by helping to build a new Catholic subculture as a viable, vital community in which committed Christians work together for the glory of God.

What follows is not a comprehensive plan of action. We mean instead to identify certain deliberate steps each of us needs to take — individual steps that, all together, will form the building blocks of a renewed Catholicism. We encourage others to add to the list or, better, compile their own lists of specifics suited to their particular circumstances and opportunities, taking as a motto a saying attributed to Saint Augustine: "In essentials, unity. In nonessentials, liberty. In all things, charity."

The steps are these:

1. Heed the universal call to holiness.
2. Discern, accept, and live out your personal vocation.
3. Rid yourself of ways of thinking and acting that smack of clericalism.
4. Do your bit to build the new Catholic subculture.
5. Encourage and contribute to a new apologetics.
6. Do apostolate.
7. Be an evangelizer.
8. Do your part in promoting and practicing shared responsibility.
9. Insist on accountability, and practice it yourself.

The order in which these points are listed isn't purely accidental — there is a kind of internal progression here. Discerning a personal vocation will lead naturally to seeking formation for apostolate, the practice of shared responsibility will involve requiring accountability of others and being accountable oneself, etc. In real life, moreover, many of these things will go on simultaneously in the lives of serious lay Catholics. For instance, someone committed to doing apostolate will almost certainly be on the lookout for opportunities to evangelize, evangelizers are sure to find themselves engaged in apologetics, and lay people who heed the universal call to holiness will contribute to the accomplishment of all the other priorities by prayer and sacrifice along with personal involvement.

Now let's take a look at our nine points.

1. HEED THE UNIVERSAL CALL TO HOLINESS.

We can hear the reaction now: "Who, *me*? A saint? You must be kidding. I'll be lucky just to squeeze into Purgatory." Maybe so. But we double down and repeat that the first, indispensable part of any layperson's contribution to revitalizing the Church must be seeking personal sanctity with courage, persistence, and entire sincerity.

For the better part of two centuries the Catholic Church in the United States rightly congratulated itself on her achievement in raising buildings to accommodate an ever-expanding network of institutions and activities: churches, rectories, convents, seminaries, colleges and universities, elementary and secondary schools, hospitals, orphanages — the list goes on and on. And together with the buildings came a vast array of groups, organizations, teams, clubs, movements, and enterprises of all sorts, not least among them publishing houses, newspapers and periodicals, and lately broadcast and digital media. And all this in order to house activities that ranged from parish bake sales and CYO basketball games to delivering babies and awarding doctoral degrees, from healing the sick and feeding the hungry to holding national conventions and Eucharistic congresses.

And all of it — or anyway very much of it — was good.

In the midst of it all, nonetheless, canny observers sometimes noted what they took to be shallowness, a lack of spiritual depth and grace-filled intensity in this vast panoply of institutional proliferation and organized activity. That was a central theme, for instance, in the fiction of the noted pre-Vatican II chronicler of American Catholicism J.F. Powers. Some of this criticism undoubtedly was unfair, even arose from envy. But it also had a measure of truth. We mention it here because spiritual superficiality is a mistake that lay Catholics can ill afford to repeat as we tackle the job of building a new subculture. Sanctity must be at its very heart.

That doesn't mean creating a new lay elite, a small number of lay-saints-in-the-making alongside a much larger body of lay-everybody-else. The idea instead is that what some might wrongly call "elitism" be the new normal for the entire body of Catholic lay people. That after all is the picture sketched by Vatican II:

> Thus it is evident to everyone, that all the faithful of Christ of whatever rank or status, are called to the fullness of the Christian life and to the perfection of charity.
>
> ...
>
> The classes and duties of life are many, but holiness is one — that sanctity which is cultivated by all who are moved by the Spirit of God, and who obey the voice of the Father and worship God the Father in spirit and in truth. These people follow the poor Christ, the humble and cross-bearing Christ in order to be worthy of being sharers in his glory.[1]

Perhaps anticipating the objection that this suggests an individualistic, self-centered version of spirituality, Vatican II adds that "by this holiness as such a more human manner of living is promoted" and calls on the laity to "be of aid to their fellow-citizens. They should raise all of society, and even creation itself, to a better mode of existence."[2] The pursuit of sanctity by each member of the Church is thus an indispensable and intrinsically outward-looking prerequisite for the other eight points in our nine-point program.

For a long time, negative attitudes toward "the world" have been an obstacle to lay spirituality. Many passages in the Bible, perhaps especially some in the Gospel of John, do indeed caution against the world and its machinations. Christian ascetical writing, from *The Imitation of Christ* to John Bunyan's seventeenth century Puritan allegory *Pilgrim's Progress*, bristles with warnings against worldly allurements. Furthermore, it would be naïve to pretend that the world in some of its aspects is not a problem, is not really an enemy of Christianity and the Christian way of life.

Taken too literally and applied too universally, however, this view of the world creates an impossible dilemma for lay people. The secular world is where we live and work, raise our families, celebrate with our friends, and experience the joys and sorrows of the human condition. Telling the laity that they must shun the world in order to be holy is like telling them to hold their breath and keep on holding it. Permanently. It doesn't work.

The tradition of *contemptus mundi* — contempt for the world — is a realistic response to what Vatican II calls the "spirit of vanity and malice which transforms into an instrument of sin those human energies intended for the service of God and man."[3] But exclusive emphasis on the danger of being corrupted has its own destructive consequences. It puts us in the position of having to disavow the law of our nature while at the same time we surrender the temporal order to the tender mercies of false ideologies and value systems radically opposed to Christianity.

Human beings are made in such a way that our choices necessarily concern human goods. That doesn't mean we never choose badly; but even when we do that, the choice is directed to some aspect of human good in what is chosen. As for good choices, proceeding from good motives and directed to the realization of human goods in ourselves and others, Vatican II assures us that, rather than passing away, they are destined to last, though in a manner we cannot now entirely comprehend:

> For after we have obeyed the Lord, and in His Spirit nurtured on earth the values of human dignity, brotherhood and freedom and indeed all the good fruits of our nature and our enterprise, we will find them again, but freed of stain, burnished and transfigured, when Christ hands over to the Father: "a kingdom eternal and universal, a kingdom of truth and life, of holiness and grace, of justice, love and peace." On this earth that Kingdom is already present in mystery. When the Lord returns it will be brought into full flower.[4]

Here is the firm basis for the conviction that ordinary, everyday life is not only the natural setting for the lives of laywomen and men but also the context in which they are to become saints. St. Josemaría Escrivá puts it like this:

> Your daily encounter with Christ takes place where your fellow men, your yearnings, your work and your affections are. It is in the midst of the most material things of the earth that we must sanctify ourselves, serving God and all mankind. … We cannot lead a double life. We cannot be like schizophrenics, if we want to be Christians. There is only one life, made of flesh and spirit.

And it is that life which has to become, in both body and soul, holy and filled with God: we discover the invisible God in the most visible and material things.[5]

Spiritual writers sometimes call this being in the world but not worldly. The key to it is prudent engagement — judging what is good in the surrounding culture, enjoying it and working to promote it, while at the same time discerning what is evil and fighting it — in oneself and also in society.

In the past, Catholics received guidance in acquiring and applying this all-important virtue, prudence, from the formation of conscience which they naturally received in their families, their parishes, and their schools. A well-formed conscience was the faculty by which, under the direction of prudence, one made moral judgments regarding the application of moral norms, transmitted to us by our parents, pastors, and teachers, to concrete situations. A conscience thus formed was something like a moral GPS — a trustworthy guide and a corrective to blind desire, not merely its enabler. While very much an individual faculty exercised individually, such a conscience was shaped by the wisdom of the Church's moral tradition.

To say times have changed now would be a gross understatement. Today Catholics must find for themselves the norms that formerly came from the now-vanished plausibility structures of the Church. Yes, the Church continues to teach and form consciences as best it can, but her effectiveness has been impaired by upheavals in society and within the Catholic world itself, including the failings of some with responsibility for teaching others. In these circumstances, each of us has a compelling need for a conscious personal relationship with Jesus, acquired and sustained in the sacraments and prayer, under the spiritual guidance of a reliable mentor.

Since this is not a handbook of lay spirituality, we won't try to spell out a plan of life for the laity. But before moving on, we do need to say a word about something that occupies a central place in most people's lives — work. By "work" we mean not only jobs and occupations but schoolwork, housework, and other productive things people do that aren't mere pastimes. Playing golf, for example, isn't work for weekend golfers, but it is for the caddie who accompanies them as well as for a pro golfer competing in a tournament.

People work for obvious practical reasons: to earn a living, support a family, contribute to the upbuilding of society, experience personal satisfaction, develop skills and acquire experience that lead to higher income and/or increased personal gratification. In his 1981 encyclical on work, *Laborem Exercens*, Saint John Paul II doesn't discount such purposes, but he does encourage us to raise our sights by identifying two other purposes that are fundamental to what he calls a Christian spirituality of work.

The first of these purposes is co-creation. John Paul explains the idea like this: "*Man*, created in the image of God, *shares by his work in the activity of the Creator* and … within the limits of his own human capabilities, man in a sense continues to develop that activity, and perfects it as he advances further and further in the discovery of the resources and values contained in the whole of creation."[6] The second purpose is participation in the redemptive work of Christ: "By enduring the toil of work in union with Christ crucified for us, man in a way collaborates with the Son of God for the redemption of humanity. He shows himself a true disciple of Christ by carrying the cross in his turn every day in the activity that he is called upon to perform."[7]

Co-creation and co-redemption: certainly these are heady concepts. But for someone who strives to interiorize them and make them his or her own, they mark out a challenging but rewarding path of sanctification in and through everyday work. To learn more, we encourage a thoughtful reading of *Laborem*

Exercens, a very rich document available in full on the Vatican web site, Vatican.va.

2. DISCERN, ACCEPT, AND LIVE OUT YOUR PERSONAL VOCATION.

Ask a Catholic what a vocation is, and chances are he or she will say, "A vocation is a calling to be a priest or a nun." These days, too, this Catholic may add, "or a deacon."

The sentiment underlying that answer is good insofar as it reflects esteem for the clerical state and the consecrated life. Yet limiting vocation to a special call that only priests, deacons, and religious women receive ignores the profoundly important reality of the unique personal vocation received by each and every baptized member of the Church — very much including the laity. We find the idea in Saint Paul's letter to the Ephesians where, speaking of Christians as the "workmanship" of God, he declares that Christians are "created in Christ Jesus for good works, which God prepared beforehand, that we should walk in them" (Eph 2:10). These "good works" which God prepares for us to perform are the substance of our personal vocations.

We find further enlightenment on personal vocation in two great sources we have cited before: St. John Henry Newman and Saint John Paul II. In a sermon titled "Divine Calls," Cardinal Newman describes personal vocation as a dynamic principle in the ongoing growth of our spiritual lives:

> We are not called once only, but many times; all through our life Christ is calling us. He called us first in baptism; but afterwards also; whether we obey his voice or not, he graciously calls us still. If we fall from our baptism, he calls us to repent; if we are striving to fulfil our calling, he calls us from grace to grace, and from holiness to holiness. ... We are all in course of calling, on and

on, from one thing to another, having no resting-place, but mounting towards our eternal rest, and obeying one command only to have another put upon us. He calls us again and again, in order to justify us again and again, — and again and again, and more and more, to sanctify and glorify us.[8]

In *Christifideles Laici*, his 1988 pastoral exhortation on the laity, Pope John Paul II also has ongoing spiritual growth in view in declaring the "fundamental objective" of lay formation to be "an ever-clearer discovery of one's vocation and the ever-greater willingness to live it."

[God] calls me and sends me forth to work for the coming of his kingdom in history. This personal vocation and mission defines the dignity and the responsibility of each member of the lay faithful and makes up the focal point of the whole work of formation, whose purpose is the joyous and grateful recognition of this dignity and the faithful and generous living-out of this responsibility.

In fact, from eternity God has thought of us and has loved us as unique individuals. Every one of us he called by name, as the Good Shepherd "calls his sheep by name" (Jn 10:3). However, only in the unfolding of the history of our lives and its events is the eternal plan of God revealed to each of us. Therefore, it is a gradual process; in a certain sense, one that happens day by day.[9]

John Paul II points to several helps by which we come to recognize our personal vocations: "receptive listening to the Word of God and the Church, fervent and constant prayer, recourse to a wise and loving spiritual guide, and a faithful discernment of the gifts and talents given by God" and how these might best be applied to the problems and opportunities we face. While certain periods in life (he mentions adolescence and young adulthood) are particularly important for vocational discernment, the pope insists that the Lord "calls *at every hour* of life" so that each of us must be continually attentive to his voice. For in the end "it is not a question of simply *knowing* what God wants. ... The individual must *do* what God wants."[10]

At the risk of making the living reality of a vocation appear overly schematized, we note what might be called vocation's three levels. First, there is the general Christian vocation that comes with baptism and is reaffirmed in confirmation: the calling to love and serve God and neighbor, and to participate in the life and work of Christ's Church. This general calling is specified by the vocation to a particular state in life — the clerical state, consecrated life, marriage, the single lay state — each with its own particular obligations and opportunities. Finally, the baptismal vocation and the state in life vocation are further specified for each individual in a personal vocation shaped by the unique, concrete circumstances of his or her life.

For a layperson to suppose only a small, select handful of people — clergy and religious — have real, honest-to-goodness callings from God is a grave obstacle to wholehearted participation in saving the Church as part of his or her personal vocation. That was illustrated by something Flannery O'Connor said when a correspondent asked her why she, a Catholic novelist and short story writer, wrote so often about Bible Belt Fundamentalist fanatics rather than her fellow Catholics. This was O'Connor's reply:

> To a lot of Protestants I know, monks and nuns are fanatics, none greater. And to a lot of the monks and nuns I know, my Protestant prophets are fanatics. For my part, I think the only difference between them is

that if you are a Catholic and have this intensity of belief you join the convent and are heard from no more;
whereas if you are a Protestant and have it, there is no
convent for you to join and you go about in the world,
getting into all sorts of trouble and drawing the wrath
of people who don't believe anything much at all down
on your head.[11]

O'Connor's response reflects the assumption, common to Catholics then and now, that "intensity of belief" must lead a Catholic
to the priesthood or religious life. Yet Flannery O'Connor herself
was a shining example of a Catholic layperson living and working in the world whose deeply held faith illuminated her art. In
the present crisis of the Church, it is more than time for Catholic
lay people, rising to the diverse challenges and opportunities of
their personal vocations, to begin — or in some cases continue
— "getting into all sorts of trouble" by witnessing to the Faith in
the face of hostile, militant secularism.

Giving witness means both walking the walk and talking
the talk — something mainstream American media seldom
allow people of faith the opportunity to do. How often do we
learn from TV or the daily newspaper that Good Samaritans
— first responders who risk and sometimes lose their lives to
save disaster victims, volunteers at homeless shelters and cen-
ters for pregnant women, generous people extending a helping
hand to others in all sorts of ways — are religious believers acting in light of their faith? How often do the media point out
that Catholic Charities is the largest private purveyor of social
services in the United States? If someone praises you for a generous act, try saying, "I do it because I'm a Catholic." It might
draw raised eyebrows, but it strengthens the Church a little and
is more honest than silence.[12]

3. RID YOURSELF OF WAYS OF THINKING AND ACTING THAT SMACK OF CLERICALISM.

Notice that we don't say, "Get rid of clericalism," as if clericalism were a pest existing somewhere outside us, to be eradicated like poison ivy in the backyard. What we are saying is, "Rid *yourself* of *your own* clericalism." And before you protest that you're the least clericalized person you know, be aware that clericalism is like old wallpaper — it's been there so long that you take it for granted, hardly see it at all, even though it continues to influence much you say and do as a Catholic. For the sake of revitalizing the Church, all of us need to look for and eliminate the clericalism *in ourselves*.

At bottom, clericalism reflects confusion about vocation: It is rooted in the unspoken assumption that the calling to the clerical state is normative for all other callings, so that the more nearly someone looks and acts like a cleric, the higher is his or her standing from a religious perspective. Some of this attitude has rubbed off on ministries performed by lay people — lector, cantor, distributor of communion, and recently catechist. These are certainly good things for laywomen and men to be. Unfortunately, however, many Catholics tend to think of them as rungs on an invisible ladder of ecclesiastical ascendancy, elevating select lay people to positions somewhat closer to the clerical ideal. That mistake is what Saint John Paul II evidently had in mind in warning that unless we're careful, the unintended consequence of lay ministries would be "clericalization" of the laity.[13]

That would be relatively harmless — a bit of ecclesiastical make-believe — were it not for the fact that clericalist thinking is an obstacle to the discernment of personal vocation. For any individual, the most important vocation is the personal calling that he or she receives from God. Priesthood is part of it for some; the lay state part of it for many others. What matters for us all is that we discern, accept, and live out our own callings.

Clericalism also has at least two other very bad practical effects. The more serious of these is the tacit encouragement it extends to lay people to ignore the universal call to holiness and settle for a second-class spirituality — being "nice" and possibly even "good" but surely not presuming to think themselves called to be "holy." The other bad result, present in everyday Church affairs, is that clericalism fosters a "Father knows best" and "Father is in charge" mentality that easily gives rise to passivity and unhealthy dependence among some lay people along with alienation among others.

Today, of course, we are experiencing what might be called the flip side of clericalist dependency. Some Catholics may still be overly dependent on directions from their clergy, but many others have swung the other way and largely ignore what the pope and bishops and pastors say — unless, that is, they commend the pope, the bishops, and the pastors for confirming an opinion they already hold or else condemn them for challenging their own comfort zones. Besides these, too, there is also a large group of people — Catholics-at-a-distance they might be called — who neither know nor care what the leaders of their Church teach even on matters that are well within their competence. Evidently there is need for a golden mean that avoids being either clericalized or anticlerical — or simply so distant from the Church that one hardly knows what it's saying or doing any more.

Rejecting clericalism doesn't mean failing to cultivate a friendly and appropriately respectful attitude toward bishops and priests or simply disregarding them. By the will of her founder, the Church in her institutional aspect is and will remain a hierarchical society with a pyramidal structure — pope at the top, then bishops, then clergy and religious, then the laity. And to paraphrase Newman, the Church would look foolish or worse if any of them were missing.

At this point, though, one may well object: "We live in America — a democracy. Why can't the Church adjust to our American way of doing things by abandoning that top-down authority structure that you describe?"

There are several answers to that. First, while no one knows exactly what the synodal Church of the future will look like (supposing it in fact becomes a reality), almost certainly her mode of decision making will be more participatory and consultative than now. Not exactly democracy perhaps, but not just top-down authority either. At the same time, however, we will still need human agents who by reason of their office are responsible, with the help of the Holy Spirit, for preserving and transmitting the core body of revealed truth entrusted to the Church — a ministry explicitly recognized by Jesus in choosing apostles, with Peter as their head, and giving them and their successors the task of preaching his message to the world until the end of time. The history of ceaseless division — and subdivision and sub-subdivision — within non-Catholic Christianity is an unhappy reminder of what happens when a religious movement lacks a Magisterium or similar teaching authority.

We also have to keep in mind that the Church's hierarchical structure is not her only dimension. The Church has a charismatic element as well — the dimension in which the Spirit dispenses graces to whom he wishes.[14] This can be seen happening in the lives of religious founders and others who, without defying the authority of ecclesiastical superiors, nevertheless found inspiration in their own Spirit-guided lights. So, too, of certain, specially gifted Catholic lay people such as Orestes Brownson, Dorothy Day, and authors Flannery O'Connor and Walker Percy.

These considerations will be increasingly important in the Church of the foreseeable future, which will have substantially fewer priests than now. The rethinking and reconfiguring of parishes may well involve situations in which one priest serves as pastor providing sacraments and pastoral services for two or more Catholic communities while a layperson — woman or man — acts as administrator of each community within the parochial cluster.[15]

Whatever form or forms dioceses and parishes actually take in the future, relationships between clergy and laity will almost certainly be substantially different — and, let's hope, far less marked by clericalism — than at present. Lay people will be obliged to take the initiative on many matters, from organizing small groups to establishing and operating schools.

If the lay initiators of such ventures wish to designate their projects as "Catholic" — a name marking them as official programs of the Church for which it takes ultimate responsibility — they will need approval from the bishop or pastor. But if they intend simply to do something within their competence on their own, without claiming official status for it and themselves accepting responsibility for the results, they can and should go ahead and do it. "Such liberty," said Pope St. John Paul II, "is a true and proper right that is not derived from any kind of 'concession' by authority, but flows from the Sacrament of Baptism, which calls the lay faithful to participate actively in the Church's communion and mission."[16]

4. DO YOUR BIT TO BUILD THE NEW CATHOLIC SUBCULTURE.

They say you can tell a congregation of American Catholics by the fact that nobody wants to sit in the front pew. While that reluctance may partly reflect a praiseworthy modesty that looks askance at even minor forms of self-advertisement, it may also testify to something not so admirable: the disinclination apparently shared by many Catholics to get too closely involved in religion.

This hesitation is the delayed fallout from the lay trustee controversy that roiled American Catholicism through much of the nineteenth century. Lay trusteeism began in several dioceses that sought to satisfy civil requirements pertaining to owning property by vesting legal ownership of parishes in laymen. Problems arose when the trustees in some places, inspired perhaps by the spirit of American-style democracy, sought to apply democratic process simplistically in an ecclesial context and claimed the right to hire and fire pastors of their choosing. One result of the bishops' long struggle with trusteeism was a lingering mistrust of lay initiatives in general. The hierarchy continued its battle with this troublesome opponent throughout the nineteenth century. And although trusteeism itself has long since disappeared, the attitudes and patterns of behavior it helped to shape are still visible in clerical hesitation to entrust the laity with responsibility, and lay hesitation in assuming it.

These ancient conflicts and their ossified offshoots must now be set aside for the sake of saving the Church. As we have said repeatedly, and don't mind saying again: Lay initiatives will be essential to building the new Catholic subculture, especially when it comes to transmitting the Faith from one generation to the next.

In the best of circumstances that will not be easy. But neither are we starting from scratch. Today's Catholics have as models the virtues of the old subculture — its tenacity, its confidence, its honest pride in being Catholic, its assertiveness and courage in creating the parochial school system as it was in its heyday. Without imagining we either can or should re-create the past, surely we can and must learn from it.

In our own day, as Rod Dreher and others who think as he does make abundantly clear, a subculture of religious inspiration will need to practice deliberate separation from the secularist worldview and its institutional and programmatic expressions in the media and public education. Confronted with secularist hostility — to say nothing of the mushy religious indifferentism so common today — Catholic distinctiveness must be planned, nurtured, matured, and promoted. Years ago, one of us provided the slogan for the first national Catholic Schools Week: "Different Where It Counts" — meaning, of course, that a truly Catholic school was different in its specifically Catholic intellectual and spiritual reality. Now the difference that sets authentically Catholic schools apart and makes them worthy of support for their academic excellence and religious authenticity must be extended to American Catholicism generally and celebrated not just one week in the year but every week year-round.

This setting of boundaries doesn't mean opening a new front in the culture war, though active resistance to secularist aggression will at times be a duty of conscience. Hallmarks of the new Catholic subculture will be things as simple, but meaningful, as displaying religious images and objects in our homes, venerating favorite saints, keeping abreast of news of the Church from the local parish to the Vatican. Additionally, the subculture will include steadily deepening our knowledge of the Faith by reading sound Catholic books and periodicals, patronizing Catholic web sites and podcasts, attending lectures, joining discussion groups, and, time permitting, taking courses offered by orthodox institutions. [17] Above all, it will involve regular attendance at Mass on Sundays, holy days, and special occasions — Ash Wednesday, the Easter Triduum, and anniversaries precious to our own families.

Spiritual and intellectual formation — including *self*-formation — of the laity will be central in the new subculture. Pardon our bluntness, but today many American Catholics are scandalously ignorant of what pertains to their Church, and matters aren't helped much by homilies that dodge timely catechetical instruction in favor of pious rambling. Lifting the dense cloud of lay ignorance is absolutely necessary and, together with serious efforts by the laity themselves, will require that bishops and pastors be consistently — even relentlessly — forthcoming with facts and figures, along with providing sound doctrinal instruction in homilies and pastoral letters.

Being part of the new Catholic subculture should not resemble membership in an exclusive private club. Membership should be open to any serious Catholic who subscribes to the saying — attributed to Saint Augustine — that we quoted above: "In essentials, unity. In nonessentials, liberty. In all things, charity." But truly accepting the authentic essentials of the Faith requires knowing what they are, and that calls for a laity well versed in the Church's doctrines, history, customs, traditions, and structures of governance.

We have a long way to go, but every reason to be optimistic in striving to build a strong, proud Catholic subculture. Anti-Catholicism in American society is no worse today than it was 100 or 150 years ago. The Church can thrive now as it did then, drawing as it has for two millennia on revealed truth and moral wisdom whose fount is Jesus. It is a matter of confidence, of commitment, of will.

5. ENCOURAGE AND CONTRIBUTE TO A NEW APOLOGETICS.

The word "apologetics" is usually taken to mean a two-fisted verbal defense of somebody or something against attacks. That apparently was the sense St. John Henry Newman had in mind when, responding to a critic who'd questioned his truthfulness, he called his classic account of his spiritual and intellectual journey to Rome *Apologia pro Vita Sua* (Apology — or better perhaps, Explanation — for His Life).

Here, though, we are using "apologetics" to refer to something slightly different, more like what the first letter of Peter has in mind in urging Christians, "Always be prepared to make a defense to any one who calls you to account for the hope that is in you," and then adding, "yet do it with gentleness and reverence"

(1 Pt 3:15). A new apologetics like this will be directed primarily not to those who might be called enemies (or at least aggressive critics) of the Catholic Church but to honest inquirers as well as wavering Catholics, in-name-only Catholics, and used-to-be Catholics.

For the most part, the agents of this new apologetics will be Catholic laywomen and men. As is often said, the best apologists are people living their ordinary lives and carrying out their ordinary duties — as husbands and wives, parents, neighbors and friends, workers — but imbuing everyday life with an unmistakable, unnamable *something* that now and then moves an observer, curious about its source (and perhaps attracted as well), to seek an "account for the hope" that is so visible in them. It's an old story, found in a source we've cited before — the Epistle to Diognetus. Writing around the year AD 200, its anonymous author remarks that his fellow Christians, who are like their fellow citizens in so many ways, nevertheless practice a way of life that "stamps it as worthy of admiration and admittedly extraordinary."[18] Today we need to do the same.

Still, good example alone can't do everything. Effective apologists must be able to give a persuasive, rational explanation of what they believe and why they believe it — something not so easy to do at a time when the Church is rife with internal tensions and conflict. Here we should remember that God gave the Church a Magisterium or teaching authority to make the distinction between essentials and nonessentials in matters of faith and morals, and thus would-be apologists need humility and tolerance. There is room in apologetics, as in the Church itself, for Catholics who emphasize social justice and Catholics for whom the life issues come first. Each group should be humble enough to honor the priorities of the other. The Church and the world need both.

The vexed question of the relationship of science and religion is a good case study of an area where intelligent Catholic apologetics is needed. Science and religion are sometimes said to be irrevocably opposed. Scientific knowledge, we're told, is the enemy of faith; the Church's condemnation of Galileo created an unbridgeable gulf between the two; and scientific advances have made it impossible for an intellectually honest person to subscribe to religious tenets today.

But none of that is true.

Saint John Paul II stated the Church's view of the matter in a 1988 letter to the director of the Vatican Observatory. While insisting that science and religion must both preserve their respective "autonomy" and "distinctiveness," he nevertheless insisted that the relationship between the two can be positive for both: "Science can purify religion from error and superstition; religion can purify science from idolatry and false absolutes. Each can draw the other into a wider world in which both can flourish." And to both he added, "You are called to learn from one another."[19]

As staff to a committee on science and human values of the bishops' national conference, one of the present writers helped organize a series of annual weekend dialogues between bishops and distinguished scientists recruited by the National Academy of Sciences and later the Congressional Research Service. Topics discussed included evolution, genetics, genetically modified organisms, stem cell research, and the relationship of brain, mind, and spirit. The format included presentations and questions, but open discussion occupied most of the three days.

With few exceptions, most of the scientists were non-Catholics while the bishops had little scientific background. The discussions were probing, often incisive, and always cordial. Agreed-upon propositions were later shared with all the U.S. bishops. These sessions not only achieved their immediate purpose — a mutual broadening of the participants' views — but also showed that the notion of an unbridgeable gulf between science and the Church is nonsense.

There is no denying science's power to describe and explain the laws of nature and provide intellectual foundation for technological achievements. But science also is inherently limited in its reach. This is especially true of the "hard" sciences that are empirical ways of coming to know, collect data on, and reason about the measurable aspects of material objects and their relationships to other objects. Material objects are not the whole of reality, and the scientific account of material objects sheds no light on the rest, including, but not limited to, aspects of mental activity and spiritual realities. Ideas, for instance, mold our world, but in themselves they have no measurable qualities and thus exist beyond science's reach.

Consider the Blessed Sacrament. A chemical analysis will find no physical change in the Eucharistic bread and wine at Mass; Catholics believe, on grounds that are reasonable though not scientific, that the bread and wine become the real, but not material, sacramental presence of Christ. Science has no way of either confirming or disproving this core Catholic belief, just as Catholics have no way of demonstrating its truth using only scientific tools.

Faith and empirical science bring to the table not only different perspectives but also positive affirmations of different though complementary realities. In practice this means the Church — or most of it anyway — lacks an adequate language for discussing the Faith with science; while science appears to suffer from a parallel deficiency when it comes to conversing with the Faith. Scientifically literate Catholics therefore have an important, overdue role to play in the new apologetics as interpreters, fostering the Church's dialogue with science in a way that deepens and enriches the understanding of reality that each brings to the table.

6. DO APOSTOLATE.

The apostolate of the laity reached its highwater mark in official approbation at the Second Vatican Council. Along with devoting part of the Dogmatic Constitution on the Church, *Lumen Gentium,* to the laity, the council issued a separate decree on the apostolate of the laity, *Apostolicam Actuositatem,* spelling out specifics of the form of lay endeavor called the lay apostolate.

Apostolicam Actuositatem (the Latin means "apostolic activity") remains even now an upbeat, forward-looking document. Declaring that the Church "can never be without" the lay apostolate, it gives an intelligent, generous introduction to the nature of lay apostolate, its purposes and forms, and its spirit. Echoing what Vatican II says about the laity in chapter four of *Lumen Gentium,* the text offers is this ringing affirmation:

> The laity must take up the renewal of the temporal order as their own special obligation. Led by the light of the Gospel and the mind of the Church, and motivated by Christian charity, they must act directly and in a definite way in the temporal sphere. As citizens they must cooperate with other citizens with their own particular skill and on their own responsibility. Everywhere and in all things they must seek the justice of God's kingdom.[20]

With an endorsement like that from such a source, you might reasonably think the apostolate of the laity had been firmly and forever firmly established in the eyes of the Church.

But if that's so, why don't we hear anything about lay apostolate now?

Vatican II ended in 1965. Within a few years, the word "apostolate" had vanished from the Catholic vocabulary, we began hearing about "ministries" for the laity instead, and discussions of lay people in right-thinking Catholic circles were focused exclusively on lay ministry. It was as if the apostolate of the laity had never existed.

What happened was far more than a semantic change. Vatican II had declared lay apostolate's fundamental goal — the "renewal of the temporal order" — to be the "special responsibility" of laywomen and men living and working in the world. Lay ministries are vastly different. At first, they only included things like being lector or cantor at Mass and distributing communion. Later, catechist was added to the list of ministries.

As time passed, however, the terms "minister" and "ministries" came to be applied to very nearly any and every function that lay people have in a parish or other church setting. The intention in this was undoubtedly good, but the implicit clericalism at work here is not. For now lay ministers are understood to be good lay people who lend a hand to busy pastors in various ways and are rewarded by being called "ministers," just a step or two removed from clerical status itself. In some circumstances, indeed, the lay ministers may get to wear cassocks and surplices so that they even *look* a bit like real clerics

And lay apostles? No one talks about them any more.

The intention here isn't to belittle lay ministers. These really are good people performing useful functions. And the need for them will only grow in the future as individual parishes are consolidated into new pastoral clusters served by a reduced number of priests, with lay people taking up some — though certainly not all — of the slack.

But the need for lay apostolate in and to the secular world also will increase in the years ahead, as will the need for a revived emphasis on recruiting and training laywomen and men for the apostolate that Vatican II declared was properly theirs. As we saw above, Cardinal Avery Dulles suggested the creation of what he called "novitiates for life" for this very purpose, and although "novitiate" may not be the best name for what's envisaged, something of the sort is indeed badly needed.

Apostolicam Actuositatem offers many illustrations of lay apostolate, and it would be easy to think of still others relating to the "renewal of the temporal order." Overall, the challenge is to bring Catholic values into settings where secularist values currently go virtually unchallenged. Without realizing it, the bishops at Vatican II anticipated the present crisis when they spoke of the "urgent need" for individual apostolate in places where "the freedom of the Church is seriously infringed" and Catholics are "few in number and widely dispersed."[21] Back in the 1960s that was an obvious reference to the Church of Silence behind the Iron and Bamboo Curtains. Today it describes the de facto position of beleaguered Christianity in the increasingly dechristianized West, not least the United States, where apostolic lay people face challenges of a magnitude and urgency not seen for centuries.

7. BE AN EVANGELIZER.

Although in modern times, as Avery Dulles points out, "evangelization has been considered the responsibility of priests and religious, assisted by a few co-opted lay volunteers," the Second Vatican Council sought to change that, insisting that all Christ's followers should take a hand in spreading the Good News. Accordingly, Dulles concludes: "In a Church that has been renewed as a community of disciples, the generality of the members will feel involved in the kind of communal and missionary existence exemplified by the first disciples of Jesus."[22]

It's a splendid vision. But what is the reality? Church leaders at the highest levels have spoken for years about a "new evangelization" arising from a fresh burst of missionary zeal in places — mainly, Europe and North America — that once were largely Christian and now are de-Christianized or well on the way to it. As far back as 1991 the American bishops published a practical guide to the new evangelization. The 2022 reorganization of the Roman Curia by Pope Francis placed evangelization at the top of the list of Vatican priorities. And as this is written, small numbers of heroic lay people here and there have committed themselves to this work.

But that's about all. There is no indication that those whom Cardinal Dulles called the "generality of the members" consider themselves obliged to lend a hand in evangelization. And meanwhile the problem of de-Christianization that evangelization is meant to address becomes ever more acute wherever the secularist culture and its powerful institutions and agents are in command.

Indeed, Western culture has become, in the words of Saint John Paul II, "disassociated not only from Christian faith but even from human values." In this crisis, he declared, there is an urgent need for lay people to be "signs of courage and intellectual creativity in the privileged places of culture, that is, the world of education — school and university — in places of scientific and technological research, the areas of artistic creativity and work in the humanities."[23]

That would be a large order in the best of circumstances, and, as we've seen, the present and foreseeable circumstances of the Church in the United States and countries like it are far from the "best" or even tolerably good. So isn't the call to evangelize asking too much of a religious body apparently on its way to becoming smaller and more culturally marginalized, with members hard pressed to keep the Faith themselves, much less spread it to others? Perhaps it is. But where a commitment to evangelization is lacking, the very existence of the Church is in question. To put it bluntly, the message to American Catholicism is evangelize or perish.

The Church of the new Catholic subculture must therefore devote far more attention to forming her members for evangelization than she now does. (Not all that hard to do, a cynic might add, considering how little time and effort are currently devoted to such formation.) Along with giving lay Catholics an honest appraisal of problems and prospects — something our clerical leaders, perhaps fearing the impact on morale of too much candor, now seldom do — homilies, formation programs, and church-sponsored media must make formation for evangelization, especially the evangelization of culture, a significant priority. The aim should be twofold: first, to make Catholics aware that they are called to be evangelizers and, second, to equip them with the tools of evangelization —something the Catholic Action movement of the pre-Vatican II years actually did with a fair degree of success.

Bishop Robert Barron recommends using the new media to make the Catholic heritage in literature, art, and music the point of entry for efforts at evangelizing culture. Journalist John Allen explains: "In a culture that's allergic to claims about truth, and resistant to moral dictates about the good, beauty still resonates, and so it's the right place to begin an evangelical appeal."[24]

That may be. But in structuring the evangelical appeal, we must remember that the Catholic Church, founded by Jesus Christ, provides essential help to people on the way to fulfillment in eternal life with God. The hard truths that are part of the Church's moral tradition and the Christian way of life — virtues and values like chastity, sobriety, self-denial, and reverence for life from conception to natural death — should not be neglected or downplayed in making this point. Contemporary men and women who've seen, and perhaps themselves experienced, the poisoned fruit of decadence and self-indulgence may actually be attracted to the Faith by gentle but firm affirmation of these moral goods.

Pointing to a hungry crowd one day, Jesus told his disciples, "You give them something to eat." They had only five loaves and two fishes, but, knowing better than to contradict Jesus, the disciples began distributing the little they had. And, to their astonishment, everyone got more than enough, and the leftovers filled twelve baskets (see Mk 6:37–44). Evangelization worth the name will always begin with a deliberate, considered commitment to obey the Lord who tells us, just as he told those first disciples, "You give them something." Having done that with the resources available to us, we can confidently, and with clear consciences, leave the rest to him.

8. DO YOUR PART IN PROMOTING AND PRACTICING SHARED RESPONSIBILITY.

In a friendly argument with a layman some years ago, a good bishop expressed doubts about the practicality of consulting lay people when engaged in decision-making. He wasn't opposed in principle, he said, but consultation was usually unworkable because it took so long to bring the laity up to speed on the complex issues Church executives often face. Yet without such remedial efforts, most lay people generally didn't understand the legal, ecclesiological, canonical, and human environments in which the Church must navigate well enough to have anything useful to say.

The bishop was right — up to a point. What he didn't recognize was that the problem he correctly identified is self-reinforcing: the longer lay people are kept in the dark about Church affairs, the harder it will become for bishops and pastors to involve them in problem-solving and the larger the laity's store of resentment is likely to grow.

The preeminent horrible example here is the cover-up of clerical sex abuse before the problem's extent finally came to light. For far too long concealment of this problem was a normal way of doing business for bishops and religious superiors who rationalized it, partly at least, on the grounds that owning up to the ugly truth would scandalize the laity. When the truth finally did come to light, the volcanic eruption of lay indignation naturally reflected not only horror at the abuse but also outrage at being kept in the dark — not least because alerting the laity to the problem earlier might well have led to earlier remedial action and therefore less harm.

Perhaps, too, the outrage partly reflected frustration over the sad fate of shared responsibility in the Church. Following Vatican II, there were bright hopes for newly established structures and processes for consulting the laity. Diocesan and parish pastoral councils sprang up left and right, and there was even serious talk of establishing a *national* pastoral council where clergy, religious, and lay people would work together to develop Church policy on issues like poverty and racism. The United States Catholic Conference (USCC), sister-organization of the National Conference of Catholic Bishops (NCCB), was established immediately after the ecumenical council in the expectation that it would evolve into such a body.

As time passed, however, interest and enthusiasm waned among clergy and laity alike. Parish and diocesan councils either disappeared completely or diminished in visibility and importance, becoming rubber-stamping bodies for decisions by bishops and pastors. Meanwhile, the Vatican turned thumbs-down on the idea of national pastoral councils. In 1997, pressured by rising costs and a widely shared feeling that the hierarchy's national structures had become too large and overbearing, the bishops folded the USCC into their episcopal conference. Today the only members of the U.S. Conference of Catholic Bishops (USCCB) are the bishops themselves, and only they can vote either in committees or general assemblies.[25]

Now, though, the tide may be turning again. With the encouragement of Pope Francis, national and diocesan synods involving broad participation by lay people have begun popping up in many places, and the "Synodal Church" is held up as an ideal. As this is written, it is too early to say with certainty what such a Synodal Church would actually look like and how it would function to avoid becoming burdened with new bureaucratic structures in a Church that already has plenty of these. "Synodality" may not be quite the same thing as "shared responsibility," but to Catholics with long memories the two things look like first cousins at least if not quite identical twins.

The International Theological Commission describes the "mentality" of synodality in their 2018 synopsis like this:

> An ecclesial mentality shaped by synodal thinking joyfully welcomes and promotes the grace in virtue of which all the baptized are qualified and called to be missionary disciples. The great challenge for pastoral conversion that follows from this for the life of the Church is to intensify the mutual collaboration of all in evangelizing witness based on everyone's gifts and roles, without clericalizing lay people and without turning the clergy into lay people, and in any case avoiding the temptation of "an excessive clericalism which keeps them [lay people] away from decision-making."[26]

Despite understandable skepticism arising from earlier disappointments, responsible lay people need to get on board the synodality bandwagon — not for synodality's sake but so that this process doesn't fall into the hands of interest groups seeking to use it as a vehicle of their own agendas. To join this particular bandwagon, however, lay people must have the education and formation that intelligent participation requires. The Catholic community in the United States already has many lay members with the natural gifts, experience, and commitment to the Church that this role requires. Get started, friends! The future is now.

9. INSIST ON ACCOUNTABILITY, AND PRAC-TICE IT YOURSELF.

The New Testament in many places calls for the practice of accountability by various categories of persons in a variety of contexts. The most direct passage — applying to everyone without exception — is in Saint Paul's letter to the Romans. Pointing out that sooner or later "we shall all stand before the judgment seat of God," Paul adds, "So each of us shall give account of himself to God" (see Rom 14:10, 12).

Accountability in its most basic sense means being answerable to some individual or group for something entrusted to you. Along the way to our final accounting to God, we all find ourselves in many intermediate situations — school, family life, work, civic affairs — where we are obliged to be accountable. And folklore and fairy tales contain many stories of failures in accountability by people who made *bad* use of something given them to hold in trust.

Typically, the narrative goes like this: A kindly fairy (or some other similarly empowered agent) grants a poor man three wishes for use in bettering his situation. But instead of choosing wisely, the foolish fellow wastes his first two wishes on bad options, so that in the end he must use his third and last wish to undo the harm he's done with the first two.

Many of us can empathize with this story and its unhappy hero for a simple reason — we've often seen something like it in real life, even made the same kind of dumb mistake ourselves, though perhaps without being fortunate enough to straighten out the mess we've made. A man inherits a large sum of money, squanders it on a costly lifestyle and bad investments, and winds up sadder and poorer, though perhaps no wiser, than he was at the start. A woman receives a terrific promotion as a manager in her company, but once given a bit of authority, she turns out to be a domineering, sharp-tongued petty tyrant who wreaks so much havoc on morale that the company's CEO has to let her go.

Episodes like these are failures in accountability. Things like inheritances and promotions carry the message, implied or specific, that those who receive them must make good use of what they've received — money, power, a position of trust — or suffer painful consequences if they don't. Often, too, accountability is a two-way street: Employees are accountable to their employers for the way they do their jobs, while employers are no less accountable to those they employ — obliged to pay them fairly, provide good benefits, and maintain healthy working conditions. And the enterprise as a whole stands to suffer if accountability is lacking on either side.

All this applies at least as much — and in some ways even more — in the Church, understood, as Vatican Council II did, as "the new People of God." She is hierarchically structured with diverse offices and roles but with all members sharing a "common dignity," "the same filial grace," "the same vocation to perfection," and "true equality" in regard to building up the Church.[27] Here, of course, our principal accountability is to Christ, the founder of the Church, who has left her future largely in our hands. But Catholics also have very serious obligations of accountability to one another — the duty of pastoral leaders to teach, pastor, and administer well; the duty of Church members to respect, obey, and support the pastors when they are engaged in the responsible exercise of their authority; and the duty to respect and support one another in living as members of the Body of Christ.

As we've seen, the worst mass failure of accountability in the Church in modern times was the sexual abuse of children and young people by some priests. In acting as they did, the guilty clergy abused not only their immediate victims but also their priesthood and the trust the Church had placed in them. And while these erring men failed miserably to live up to what others rightly expected of them, so too did the bishops and religious superiors who concealed the priests' misdeeds while allowing them to remain in ministry. How are we to explain what happened? Clericalism played a large part in it — not as a cause of the perverse sexual behavior, which had its roots deep in the psyches of the abusers, but as an enabler, propping up a failed system of priestly accountability and hierarchical oversight by persistent concealment.

As the Church — that is to say, all of us — continues to pay a price for what happened, a cost measured not only in dollars and cents but also in public esteem and trust, the lessons of this terrible episode must not be lost. Revitalizing the Church as it enters long years of shrinkage and radical institutional change will require an across-the-board change of mentality on the part of all members, from the pope on down. For the laity, that will mean shedding clericalized habits of passivity and dependency that lead them to see themselves as spectators rather than fully engaged participants in the Church's great work of spreading the Good News of Christ. In this way, and no other, the Church of the future will emerge from this present crucible as a community of accountability grounded in faith, hope, and love.

• • •

Although we called this chapter "Building a Cathedral," readers will have noticed the absence of blueprints and architectural drawings — no detailed descriptions of how to structure the Church of the future and the new Catholic subculture. The reason is simple: we don't know. We take it for granted that the Church in, say, the year 2075 will still have her fundamental hierarchical structure since that is how Christ intends it. We assume, too, that there will be much more consultation of the laity than now, although whether we will then be calling the Church "synodal" or will have found some less esoteric word for it remains to be seen. Beyond those broad hints, we think it's prudent to leave the design of the Church half a century from now to time and the Holy Spirit. They will have the last word anyway.

What we have done is call attention to attitudes and ways of acting that Catholic laywomen and men need to adopt (or reaffirm and develop further, if they've already adopted them) in order to play their part in preserving and renewing their Church: seek holiness, discern and live their personal vocations, avoid clericalism, evangelize, and practice the other items listed above. Some words of Archbishop Charles Chaput sum up what we have in mind: "The vocation of a Christian disciple is to feed the soul as well as the mind; to offer the world a vision of men and women made whole by the love of God, the knowledge of creation, and the reality of things unseen; to see the beauty of the world in the light of eternity; to recapture the nobility of the human story, and the dignity of the human person."[28] If we Catholic lay people do all that, we will be preparing ourselves for our part in revitalizing our Church. Come to think of it, we may even build a cathedral or two.

Afterword

There is a pleasure in being in a ship beaten about by a storm, when we are sure that it will not founder. The persecutions which harass the Church are of this nature.

— Blaise Pascal

Pascal, a French religious thinker and mathematician of the seventeenth century, was right then and is no less right today. The present crisis of the Church is an occasion for neither panic nor despair. Along with much to distress us, the Catholic Church's current situation contains real reasons for hope, provided we have the courage and creativity to recognize and take advantage of them.

At certain points in this book we have cited three very different thinkers — Rod Dreher, Charles Taylor, and Pope St. John Paul II. Nearing the end, we turn to them again in order to draw together the threads of the program by which Catholic lay people can position themselves to meet the challenges that lie ahead.

Rod Dreher is a feisty conservative writer who in two widely noted books, *The Benedict Option* (2017) and *Live Not By Lies* (2020), makes a forceful case for one approach. He argues that faithful Christians in the United States are under assault from the "soft totalitarianism" of secularist progressivism promoted by sympathetic media, compliantly "woke" universities and corporations, and internet giants like Facebook, Apple, Microsoft, and Google.[1] In response, Dreher calls for the creation of communities of like-minded believers as an essential survival strategy. "Nobody but the most deluded of the old-school Religious Right believes that this cultural revolution can be turned back," he writes. "Rather than wasting energy and resources fighting unwinnable political battles, we should instead work on building communities, institutions, and networks of resistance that can outwit, outlast, and eventually overcome the occupation."[2]

Charles Taylor, professor emeritus of philosophy at McGill University in Montreal, is the author of two acclaimed studies, *Sources of the Self* (1989) and *A Secular Age* (2007). In 2007 he was awarded the prestigious Templeton Prize in religion. In *A Secular Age* he speaks of secularism as a historical given but argues that people of faith can and should have a crucial role in this secularized world:

> The goal in this case is not to return to an earlier formula ... but inevitably and rightly Christian life today will look for and discover new ways of moving beyond the present orders to God. One could say that we look for new and unprecedented itineraries. Understanding our time in Christian terms is partly to discern these new

paths, opened by pioneers who have discovered a way through the particular labyrinthine landscape we live in, its thickets and trackless wastes, to God.[3]

So, who is right, Dreher or Taylor?

The answer is clear: Both.

Dreher is right in pointing to a grave present challenge directed against religious faith by militant atheism and its powerful agents and collaborators in American secularist culture. The Christian response, he correctly argues, requires networks of groups and institutions — the new Catholic subculture that we have sketched here is such a network — within which believers can celebrate and practice their faith, transmit it to the next generation, and engage in evangelization to the extent that evangelization is a possibility in a cultural environment dominated by hostile secularism.

Dreher, whose own religious trajectory has taken him from Methodism through Roman Catholicism to Orthodoxy, is addressing an interdenominational audience of faithful Christians. We, however, are speaking in this book directly to Catholics, and we believe strongly that it is necessary for the Catholic subculture and its institutions to be clearly, unequivocally *Catholic*. On that basis, fruitful ecumenical relations with other faithful Christians will be both possible and desirable.

Taylor is right in saying people of faith will have a crucial role in the secularized world, although one likely to take them by "unprecedented itineraries" to the ultimate goal, which is union with God.[4] This vision finds resonance in the vision of Joseph Ratzinger that we cited earlier, according to which the Catholic Church of the future, having passed through this time of trial, will be a beacon to people searching for the meaning of life.

And, finally, in the end Pope St. John Paul II is right when he depicts the important part that the Catholic laity can and must have in revitalizing the Church — first of all, preserving it, of course, and then transmitting it to others as a viable and inviting community of faith — and thus, helping to save the world by rescuing it from the deadly aridity of being a place without faith, hope, and love. The Holy Father writes:

> There cannot be two parallel lives in their existence: on the one hand, the so-called "spiritual" life, with its values and demands; and on the other, the so-called "secular" life, that is, life in a family, at work, in social relationships, in the responsibilities of public life and in culture. The branch, engrafted to the vine which is Christ, bears its fruit in every sphere of existence and activity. In fact, every area of the lay faithful's lives, as different as they are, enters into the plan of God, who desires that these very areas be the "places in time" where the love of Christ is revealed and realized for both the glory of the Father and service of others. Every activity, every situation, every precise responsibility — as, for example, skill and solidarity in work, love and dedication in the family and the education of children, service to society and public life and the promotion of truth in the area of culture — are the occasions ordained by Providence for a "continuous exercise of faith, hope and charity."[5]

That, briefly stated, is the program for revitalizing the Church that we propose.

Books Every Catholic Should Read

Almost by definition, a well-informed Catholic is a well-read Catholic. Here is a list of books that, ideally, every Catholic will be familiar with. Many other books also are well worth reading, but this list should help in getting started.

REFERENCE

The Catechism of the Catholic Church. 2nd ed. Washington, DC: United States Catholic Conference, Inc., 1994.

Flannery, Austin, ed. *Vatican Council II: The Conciliar and Post Conciliar Documents.* Northport, NY: Costello Publishing, 1988.

The New Testament. Recommended for translation (RSV, in both cases) and notes: *The Navarre Bible: New Testament*, Princeton, New Jersey: Scepter Publishers, 2001; and *New Testament Ignatius Catholic Study Bible*, RSV Second Catholic Edition, San Francisco: Ignatius Press, 2010.

HISTORY

Burleigh, Michael. *Earthly Powers: The Clash of Religion and Politics in Europe, from the French Revolution to the Great War.* New York: HarperCollins, 2007.

———. *Sacred Causes: The Clash of Religion and Politics, from the Great War to the War on Terror.* New York: HarperCollins, 2008.

Duffy, Eamon. *Saints and Sinners: A History of the Popes.* 4th ed. London: Yale University Press, 2014.

Hitchcock, James. *History of the Catholic Church: From the Apostolic Age to the Third Millennium.* San Francisco: Ignatius Press, 2012.

Morris, Charles R. *American Catholic: The Saints and Sinners Who Built America's Most Powerful Church.* New York: Random House Times Books,1997.

BIOGRAPHY AND AUTOBIOGRAPHY

Saint Augustine. *Confessions.* Translated by R.S. Pine-Coffin. London: Penguin Classics, 1961.

Day, Dorothy. *The Long Loneliness: The Autobiography of the Legendary Catholic Social Activist.* New York: HarperOne, 2009.

Newman, John Henry. *Apologia Pro Vita Sua.* Edited by Ian Ker. New York: Penguin Classics, 1995.

Sheen, Fulton J. *Treasure in Clay: The Autobiography of Fulton J. Sheen.* New York: Image Books/Doubleday, 1982.

St. Teresa of Avila, *Autobiography of St. Teresa of Avila.* Translated and edited by E. Allison Peers. Mineola, NY: Dover Publications, Inc., 2010.

St. Thérèse of Lisieux, *The Story of a Soul: The Autobiography of Saint Thérèse of Lisieux.* Translated by John Clarke. 3rd ed. Washington, DC: ICS Publications, 1996.

Weigel, George. *Witness to Hope*: *The Biography of Pope John Paul II*. New York: Harper Perennial, 2005.

SPIRITUAL LIFE

Escrivá, Josemaría. *Christ Is Passing By: Homilies.* New York: Scepter Publishers, 1974.

St. Francis de Sales. *Philothea or An Introduction to the Devout Life.* Gastonia, NC: Tan Classics, 2010.

Thomas à Kempis. *The Imitation of Christ.* Dover Books, 2013.

THEOLOGY AND CATECHETICS

Chesterton, G.K. *The Everlasting Man.* San Francisco: Ignatius Press, 2008.

Guardini, Romano. *The Lord.* Washington, DC: Regnery, 1996.

Lewis, C.S. *Mere Christianity.* New York: HarperOne, 2015.

Ratzinger, Joseph. *Introduction to Christianity*. San Francisco: Ignatius Press, 2004.

LITERATURE

Alighieri, Dante. *The Divine Comedy: Inferno; Purgatorio; Paradiso.* Translated by Allen Mandelbaum. London: Everyman's Library, 1995.

Bernanos, Georges. *The Diary of a Country Priest.* Cambridge, MA: Da Capo Press, 2002.

Greene, Graham. *The Power and the Glory.* New York: Penguin Classics, 2015.

Manzoni, Alessandro. *The Betrothed.* Translated by Michael F. Moore. New York: Modern Library, 2022.

Undset, Sigrid. *Kristin Lavransdatter.* Translated by Tiina Nunnally. New York: Penguin Classics, 2005.

Waugh, Evelyn. *Brideshead Revisited.* New York: Back Bay Books / Little, Brown, and Company, 2012.

Notes

CHAPTER 1: WHY THE LAITY MUST SAVE THE CHURCH

1. John Henry Newman, *On Consulting the Faithful in Matters of Doctrine* (New York: Sheed & Ward, 1961), 75–76.

2. Ibid., 77.

3. Ryan Burge, "How America's Youth Lost Its Religion in 1990s," Religion News Service, April 13, 2022.

4. John L. Ronsvalle and Sylvia Ronsvalle, *The State of Church Giving Through 2018: What If Jesus Comes Back in 2025?* (Champaign, IL: empty tomb, inc., 2021), 128.

5. Brad S. Gregory, *The Unintended Reformation: How a Religious Reformation Secularized Society* (Cambridge, MA: The Belknap Press of Harvard University Press, 2012), 160.

6. Charles Taylor, *A Secular Age* (Cambridge, MA: The Belknap Press of Harvard University Press, 2007), 12.

7. Orestes Brownson, "Catholic Polemics" in *Brownson Reader: A Selection of the Writings of Orestes A. Brownson*, Alvan S. Ryan, ed. (New

York: P.J. Kenedy & Sons, 1955), 334–335.

8. Carl R. Trueman, "The Failure of Evangelical Elites," *First Things*, November 2021, 44–45. https://www.firstthings.com/article /2021/11/the-failure-of-evangelical-elites.

9. Jacques Maritain, *Three Reformers: Luther, Descartes, Rousseau* (New York: Apollo Editions, 1970), 27.

10. Alasdair MacIntyre, *A Short History of Ethics: A History of Moral Philosophy from the Homeric Age to the Twentieth Century* (New York: Macmillan, 1966), 122

11. Paul Hacker, *Faith in Luther: Martin Luther and the Origin of Anthropocentric Religion* (Steubenville, Ohio: Emmaus Academic, 2017), 10.

12. Ibid., 23.

13. Maritain, *Three Reformers*, 99.

14. MacIntyre, *Short History of Ethics,* 122.

15. Taylor, *A Secular Age*, 206.

16. Ibid., 207.

17. Ryszard Legutko, a Polish philosopher and political figure who has experienced both communism and liberal democracy on the European Union model and finds fundamental likenesses between them, writes: "The need for building a liberal-democratic society thus implies the withdrawal of the guarantee of freedom for those whose actions and interests are said to be hostile to what the liberal democrats conceive as the cause of freedom." Ryszard Legutko, *The Demon in Democracy: Totalitarian Temptations in Free Societies* (New York: Encounter Books, 2016), 20.

18. Taylor, *A Secular Age*, 379.

19. Matthew Arnold, "Dover Beach," lines 21, 33–34.

20. Edmund Gosse, *Father and Son* (New York: Oxford University Press, 2004), 185–186. Gosse reproduces the whole of this letter near the end of his book; his treatment of the elder Gosse remained respectful, indeed loving, throughout.

21. For a short account of Modernism and Pope Pius X's response

to it see Russell Shaw, *American Church: The Remarkable Rise, Meteoric Fall, and Uncertain Future of Catholicism in America* (San Francisco: Ignatius Press, 2013), 51–55. For a book-length study, see Marvin R. O'Connell, *Critics on Trial: An Introduction to the Catholic Modernist Crisis* (Washington, D.C.: The Catholic University of America Press, 1994).

22. Frederich Nietzsche, *On the Genealogy of Morals* and *Ecce Homo*, Walter Kaufmann editor (New York: Random House, 1967), 334.

23. William L. Shirer, *The Rise and Fall of the Third Reich: A History of Nazi Germany* (New York: Simon & Schuster, 1990), 100.

24. Georg Zachariae, *Mussolini si confessa* (Milano: Garzanti, 1948), 25.

25. John Paul II, *Dominum et Vivificantem*, vatican.va, par. 56.

26. Henry Adams, *The Education of Henry Adams* (New York: Random House Modern Library, 1931), 34.

27. Planned Parenthood of Southeastern Pennsylvania v. Casey, 505 U.S. 833, 851 (1992).

28. Alasdair MacIntyre, *After Virtue*, 3rd ed. (Notre Dame, IN: University of Notre Dame Press, 2008), 250–251, 253.

29. Quoted in Ian Ker, *John Henry Newman* (Oxford: Oxford University Press, 1990), 479.

CHAPTER 2: THE AMERICAN CHURCH

1. James Gibbons, "The Roman Sermon of the American Cardinal on Church and State in the United States, March 25, 1887" in John Tracy Ellis, ed., *Documents of American Catholic History* (Milwaukee: The Bruce Publishing Company, 1962), 458.

2. Gibbons and his friends responded respectfully by assuring Pope Leo they held none of the condemned views. Although now customarily dismissed by critics sympathetic to the Americanizers' position, the papal document was prescient in warning against things like promoting activism over contemplation in the religious life and

claiming direct personal inspiration by the Holy Spirit as justification for unapproved innovations.

3. Marvin R. O'Connell, *John Ireland and the American Catholic Church* (St. Paul, MN: Minnesota Historical Society Press, 1988), 274ff.

4. James Hennesey, *American Catholics: A History of the Roman Catholic Community in the United States* (New York: Oxford University Press, 1981), 187. See also Jessica A. Greene and Joseph M. O'Keefe, "Enrollment in Catholic Schools in the United States" in *Handbook of Research on Catholic Education*, ed. Thomas C. Hunt, Ellis A. Joseph, and Ronald J. Nuzzi (Westport, CT: Greenwood Press, 2001), 162.

5. Hennesey, *American Catholics,* 323. See also Greene and O'Keefe, "Enrollment," 162, and Thomas D. Snyder, ed., *120 Years of American Education: A Statistical Portrait*, (National Center for Education Statistics, 1993) 49, table 15. https://nces.ed.gov/pubs93/93442.pdf.

6. Charles R. Morris, *American Catholic: The Saints and Sinners Who Built America's Most Powerful Church* (New York: Random House Times Books, 1997), vi.

7. John Courtney Murray, *We Hold These Truths: Catholic Reflections on the American Proposition* (New York: Sheed and Ward, 1960), 30.

8. Ibid., 273–294.

9. Lyman R. Stone, "America Loses Religion, Somewhat," *National Review*, June 14, 2021. https://www.nationalreview.com/magazine/2021/06/14/america-loses-religion-somewhat/.

10. Ibid.

11. *The Benedict Option: A Strategy for Christians in a Post-Christian Nation* (New York: Sentinel, 2017), 17.

12. "Frequently Requested Church Statistics," Center for Applied Research in the Apostolate, https://cara.georgetown.edu/faqs.

13. The number of marriage annulments initiated also has declined, from 60,691 in 1985 to 19,497 in 2019. When, several years ago, one of the present writers congratulated a tribunal official in a large diocese on what he supposed was evidence of a decline in the rate of marital breakdown among Catholics, the tribunal official

replied that it was nothing of the sort. Catholic marriages were still breaking down at a great rate, he said, but fewer Catholics in broken marriages sought annulments, preferring instead simply to get divorced and enter into new marriages — or cohabit — outside the Church.

14. Ralph Martin, *A Church in Crisis: Pathways Forward* (Steubenville, OH: Emmaus Road Publishing, 2020), 238.

15. Ross Douthat, "Catholic Ideas and Catholic Realities: On Populists, Integralists, Benedictines, and Tradinistas," *First Things*, (August/September, 2021), https://www.firstthings.com/article/2021/08/catholic-ideas-and-catholic-realities.

16. Stephen Bullivant, *Mass Exodus: Catholic Disaffiliation in Britain and America Since Vatican II* (New York: Oxford University Press, 2020), 17. Here as elsewhere we turn to Bullivant's analysis because it is recent, accords with the obvious facts as they are known to us, and steers clear of the ideological special pleading found in some other accounts of these events.

17. Ibid., 131.

18. For an overview of this, see Shaw, *American Church*, 63–118.

19. Bullivant, *Mass Exodus*, 263. Citing Mary Douglas, *Natural Symbols: Explorations in Cosmology* (London: Routledge, 1996), 44.

20. Robert Royal, *A Deeper Vision: The Catholic Intellectual Tradition in the Twentieth Century* (San Francisco: Ignatius Press, 2015), 587.

21. Charles J. Chaput, *Strangers in a Strange Land: Living the Catholic Faith in a Post-Christian World* (New York: Henry Holt and Company, 2017), 5.

22. Ibid.

23. In quoting this comment, we are not making a blanket condemnation of Catholic on-campus programs. Campus ministry may be doing great work elsewhere. At this professor's school, nevertheless, the Church's ministry to young Catholics was a clear case of go-along-to-get-along Catholicism.

24. Bill Donohue, *The Truth About Clergy Sexual Abuse: Clarifying*

the Facts and the Causes (San Francisco: Ignatius Press, 2021), 7ff.

25. Bullivant, *Mass Exodus*, 234.

26. Germain Grisez, *The Way of the Lord Jesus*, vol. 1, *Christian Moral Principles* (Chicago: Franciscan Herald Press, 1983), 552.

27. Joseph Ratzinger cited in Tod Worner, "When Father Joseph Ratzinger Predicted the Future of the Church," *Voices and Views, Aleteia,* June 13, 2016, www.aleteia.org/2016/06/13/when-cardinal -joseph-ratzinger-predicted-the-future-of-the-church.

CHAPTER 3: THREE VERSIONS OF THE FUTURE

1. Mary Eberstadt, *It's Dangerous to Believe: Religious Freedom and Its Enemies* (New York: HarperCollins, 2016), xi.

2. Ibid., x–xi.

3. Ibid., 33. Here we might note that some of the responsibility for the success of the sexual revolution may lie with decent people whose reaction to this assault on values to which they subscribed was simply to go on "minding their own business" instead of putting up resistance.

4. One might also add the name of Karl Marx, since he and early Marxists advocated free love as a way of releasing women from the bonds of matrimony, motherhood, and family. The approach was introduced in Russia after the Bolshevik revolution along with unilateral divorce, legalized pornography and abortion, acceptance of homosexual relations, and the collectivization of children. Stalin, finding the results socially disruptive, eventually returned to less radical policies.

5. Piotr Mazurkiewicz, "The Cultural Roots of the Clergy Sexual Misconduct Crisis" in *Clerical Sexual Misconduct: An Interdisciplinary Analysis*, ed. Jane F. Adolphe and Ronald J. Rychlak (Providence, RI: Cluny Media, 2020), 133.

6. A recent historian of American Catholicism says "a Chicago pastor" reported in 1933 that more than half of Catholic married couples were practicing contraception, although, the same writer adds,

that likely was an exaggeration. A 1952 poll found 51% of Catholics did not consider "mechanical birth control" seriously sinful; and a 1960 survey, presumably reflecting the recent introduction of oral contraception — the Pill — found that 38% of Catholic wives were using some form of contraceptive. See Leslie Woodcock Tentler, *American Catholics: A History* (New Haven: Yale University Press, 2020), 236–238.

7. Ralph Martin, *A Church in Crisis,* 238.

8. "Frequently Requested Statistics," CARA.

9. The 2019 figure was the lowest since 1995. The figures had actually risen after that, reaching 553 in 2005. Presumably the numerical decline occurring thereafter reflects closings and consolidations of parishes.

10. Wilton Gregory, "To Address Ongoing Decline in Religious Participation, Church Must Tell the Truth, Return to Its Central Mission," *Catholic Standard*, April 15, 2021, Voices, https://cathstan.org /voices/cardinal-wilton-gregory/to-address-ongoing-decline-in -religious-participation-church-must-tell-the-truth-return-to-its -central-mission.

11. David M. Byers and Bernard Quinn, *New Directions for the Rural Church: Case Studies in Area Ministry* (Mahwah, NJ: Paulist Press, 1978).

12. For instance: in early 2022, Dr. Päivi Räsänen, a conservative Christian member of the Finnish parliament who is a physician and former minister of the interior, was tried in Helsinki, charged with "hate speech" for opposing same-sex marriage on the basis of scriptural teaching. The court eventually ruled in her favor, but who is to say there won't be more such cases, with quite different outcomes? Court cases of a similar kind lately have cropped up in several places in the United States. See Mark A. Kellner, "Christian Member of Finnish Parliament on Trial for 'Hate Speech' on Gays," *The Washington Times*, January 24, 2022, World, https://www.washingtontimes.com /news/2022/jan/24/christian-member-finnish-parliament

-trial-hate-spe/.

13. Eberstadt, *It's Dangerous to Believe*, xx.

14. Romano Guardini, *The End of the Modern World* (Wilmington, DE: ISI Books, 2001), 210.

15. Ibid.,94.

16. Dreher, *Benedict Option*, 9. On the decision, see *Obergefell v. Hodges 576 U.S. 644* (2015). The Supreme Court split 5-4 in deciding the case, with Associate Justice Anthony Kennedy writing the majority opinion in which Justices Ginsburg, Breyer, Sotomayor, and Kagan joined, while Chief Justice Roberts and Justices Scalia, Thomas, and Alito dissented.

17. Dreher, *Benedict Option* , 2.

18. Ibid., 95.

19. Avery Dulles, *Models of the Church*, expanded edition (New York: Doubleday Image Book, 2002), 210.

20. Ibid., 210–211.

21. David Brooks, "The Benedict Option," *The New York Times,* March 14, 2017, Opinion, https://www.nytimes.com/2017/03/14 /opinion/the-benedict-option.html.

22. Susan Orr Traffas, "A Bad Catholic's Guide to Good Politics: Looking at the Benedict Option through American Eyes," *Fellowship of Catholic Scholars Quarterly 41*, no.2 (Summer 2018):158. https://www .catholicscholars.org/PDFFiles/v41n2sum2018.pdf

23. See William Bradford, "Of Plymouth Plantation" in *The Mayflower Papers* (New York: Penguin Books, 2007), 99.

24. Traffas, "Bad Catholic's Guide to Good Politics," 158.

25. Dulles, *Models of the Church*, 199, 203. As Cardinal Dulles undoubtedly was aware, there also were backsliders among these early Christians who, at times of persecution, succumbed to pressure and saved themselves by offering the symbolic pinch of incense to the pagan deities. At the same time, though, others refused to give in. This was indeed an age of martyrs, although when put to the test not everyone opted for martyrdom.

26. Ibid., 205.

27. "The Epistle to Diognetus," in *Readings in Church History*, vol. 1, *From Pentecost to the Protestant Revolt*, ed. Colman J. Barry (Westminster, MD: The Newman Press, 1960), 39–40.

28. Josemaría Escrivá, "Passionately Loving the World," in *In Love with the Church*, Josemaría Escrivá: A Website Dedicated to the Writings of Opus Dei's Founder (1902–1975), par. 52, 54, www.escrivaworks.org.

29. Bullivant, *Mass Exodus*, 240.

30. Christian Smith and Amy Adamczyk, *Handing Down the Faith: How Parents Pass Their Religion on to the Next Generation* (New York: Oxford University Press, 2021), 224–225.

31. Ibid., 99, table 4.3.

32. Ibid., 113, table 4.11.

33. Ibid., 225.

34. Brian D. Ray, "Research Facts on Homseschooling," National Home Education Research Institute, September 15, 2022, https://www.nheri.org/research-facts-on-homeschooling/.

35. Pierce v. Society of Sisters, 268 U.S. 510, 534–535 (1925). The case arose in Oregon and concerned a statute called the Oregon Compulsory Education Act. Among groups promoting this measure were the Orange Society and the Ku Klux Klan. The Supreme Court's unanimous decision was delivered on June 1, 1925, with the opinion written by Associate Justice James C. McReynolds.

36. R. R. Reno, "Omaha," *First Things*, (June 2021), https://www.firstthings.com/article/2021/06/omaha.

37. Ian Lundquist, "Classical Schools in Modern America," *National Affairs*, (Fall 2019) https://www.nationalaffairs.com/publications/detail/classical-schools-in-modern-america.

38. As this is written, the nation is reeling at news of a teenage shooter who was detected checking out suppliers of ammunition on his hand-held device shortly before he killed several schoolmates with a handgun.

39. Robert Barron and John L. Allen, Jr., *To Light a Fire on the Earth: Proclaiming the Gospel in a Secular Age* (New York: Image Books, 2017), 246.

40. Paul Soukup, "Essay 1: Digital Culture and Religious Education" in "A Debate between Paul Soukup, SJ, and Paul Glader on How Digital Culture Is Affecting Media Education on Religion," *Church, Communication and Culture*, 5, no. 2, (2020): 148. https://doi.org /10.1080/23753234.2020.1765698.

CHAPTER 4: BUILDING A CATHEDRAL

1. Vatican Council II, *Lumen Gentium*, vatican.va, par. 40–41.

2. Ibid.

3. Vatican II, *Gaudium et Spes*, vatican.va, par. 37.

4. Ibid., 39, citing Preface for the Feast of Christ the King.

5. Escrivá "Passionately Loving the World," par. 52.

6. John Paul II, *Laborem Exercens*, vatican.va, par. 25. Italics in original.

7. Ibid., par. 27.

8. John Henry Newman, "Divine Calls," in *Parochial and Plain Sermons* (San Francisco: Ignatius Press, 1987), 1569–1570.

9. John Paul II, *Christifideles Laici*, vatican.va, par. 58.

10. Ibid. Italics in original.

11. Flannery O'Connor to Sister Mariella Gable, Midgeville, May 4, 1963, in *Flannery O'Connor: Collected Works*, ed. Sally Fitzgerald (New York: The Library of America, 1988), 1183.

12. For more about personal vocation, see Germain Grisez and Russell Shaw, *Personal Vocation: God Calls Everyone by Name* (Huntington, IN: Our Sunday Visitor, 2003).

13. John Paul II, *Christifideles Laici*, par. 23.

14. Jesus speaks of this during his encounter with Nicodemus, the inquiring Pharisee: "The wind blows where it wills … so it is with every one who is born of the Spirit" (Jn 3:8).

15. Something like this is already starting to emerge in a number

of U.S. dioceses. In 2021, for example, the Archdiocese of Cincinnati, anticipating fewer priests and declining lay participation, announced a restructuring that would start by grouping its 208 parishes into 57 "families" of parishes sharing pastors, staff, and infrastructure while initially remaining canonically independent. Other dioceses have carried out similar programs for clustering parishes or are considering them.

16. John Paul II, *Christifideles Laici*, par. 29.

17. Two distance learning sources well worth looking into: the Catholic Distance University and the Saint John Paul II Institute at Houston's University of Saint Thomas. We also include as an appendix to this book a short, by no means exhaustive, list of books that every Catholic ought to read.

18. "The Epistle to Diognetus" in *Readings in Church History*, 39.

19. John Paul II to Rev. George V. Coyne, Vatican, June 1, 1988, vatican.va.

20. Vatican II, *Apostolicam Actuositatem*, vatican.va, par. 7.

21. Ibid., 17.

22. Dulles, *Models of the Church*, 212.

23. John Paul II, *Christifideles Laici*, par. 44.

24. Barron and Allen, *To Light a Fire on the Earth*, 248.

25. Non-bishops do serve as USCCB consultants and staff but authority in the organization rests exclusively with the bishops. Previously, in the days of NCCB-USCC, non-bishops had been full, voting members of USCC's policy-formulating committees.

26. International Theological Commission, *Synodality in the Life and Mission of the Church*, vatican.va, par.104, citing Francis *Evangelii Gaudium*, par. 102.

27. *Lumen Gentium*, par. 9, 32.

28. Charles J. Chaput, "Fire Upon the Earth," *First Things*, (May 2022) https://www.firstthings.com/article/2022/05/fire-upon-the-earth.

AFTERWORD

1. Rod Dreher, "The Road to Soft Totalitarianism: How the Managerial Class Will Use Anarchy to Justify Tyranny," *The American Conservative*, Live Not By Lies, June 1, 2020, https://www .theamericanconservative.com/anarcho-tyranny-road-to-soft -totalitarianism/.

2. Dreher, *The Benedict Option*, 12.

3. Taylor, *A Secular Age*, 755.

4. Ibid.

5. John Paul II, *Christifideles Laici*, par. 59, citing *Apostolicam Actuositatem*, 4.

About the Authors

David M. Byers has ministered within the Catholic Church as a lay employee of the Glenmary Home Missioners, a religious community that serves mission dioceses in the United States and its dependencies (1973–78); as senior staff to the U.S. Conference of Catholic Bishops with responsibilities for the home missions, world mission, evangelization, and the relationship of religion and science (1978–2007); as a founding director of the National Catholic Partnership on Disability (1982–94); as a planning consultant to the Diocese of Salina (2008–10); and as a parish volunteer in many capacities. Byers holds a doctorate in English from the University of Minnesota. He and Pat, his wife of 53 years, live in the Washington, DC, suburbs.

Russell Shaw was Secretary for Public Affairs of the National Conference of Catholic Bishops/United States Catholic Conference from 1969 to 1987 and Director of Information of the Knights of Columbus from 1987 to 1997. His many books include *American Church* (Ignatius, 2013), *Eight Popes and the Crisis of Modernity* (Ignatius, 2020), and *The Life of Jesus Christ* (Our Sunday Visitor, 2021). He has BA and MA degrees from Georgetown University and received an honorary Doctorate of Humane Letters from The Catholic University of America in 2019. A widower, he has five children, ten grandchildren, and (for the present) two great-grandchildren.